FACING THE DRAGON

ALSO BY ROBERT L. MOORE

John Wesley and Authority: A Psychological Perspective

The Archetype of Initiation: Sacred Space, Ritual Process, and Personal Transformation

The Magician and the Analyst: The Archetype of the Magus in Occult Spirituality and Jungian Analysis

with J. Gordon Melton

The Cult Experience: Responding to the New Religious Pluralism

with Douglas Gillette

King, Warrior, Magician, Lover: Rediscovering the Archetypes of the Mature Masculine

The King Within: Accessing the King in the Male Psyche

The Warrior Within: Accessing the Knight in the Male Psyche

The Magician Within: Accessing the Shaman in the Male Psyche

The Lover Within: Accessing the Lover in the Male Psyche

edited by Robert L. Moore

Sources of Vitality in American Church Life

Anthropology and the Study of Religion (with Frank Reynolds)

Jung's Challenge to Contemporary Religion (with Murray Stein)

Carl Jung and Christian Spirituality

Jung and Christianity in Dialogue: Faith, Feminism, and Hermeneutics (with Daniel J. Meckel)

Self and Liberation: The Jung-Buddhism Dialogue (with Daniel J. Meckel)

Robert L. Moore

FACING THE DRAGON
Confronting Personal and Spiritual Grandiosity

Edited by Max J. Havlick, Jr.

Chiron Publications
Wilmette, Illinois

Book and cover design by Peter Altenberg.
Printed in the United States of America.
Fourth printing   2009

Library of Congress Cataloging-in-Publication Data
Moore, Robert L.
    Facing the dragon : confronting personal and spiritual grandiosity / Robert L. Moore ; edited by Max J. Havlick, Jr.
        p. cm.
Includes bibliographical references and index.
    ISBN 978-1-888602-21-0 (alk. paper)
    1. Jungian psychology. 2. Narcissism. 3. Megalomania. 4. Good and evil—Psychological aspects. 5. Secularism. 6. Psychoanalysis and religion. 7. Jung, C. G. (Carl Gustav), 1875-1961—Religion. I. Havlick, Max J. II. Title.
BF173.J85 M67 2003
150.19'54—dc21

                            2002151396

Drawings by Michael A. Finnegan, a Chicago-area artist and musician who paints fantasy, dreamscapes, and landscape surrealism, and whose music follows the same style: "The Big Smile" (chapter 1); "Woman at Risk" (chapter 5); "Dragon and Friend" (chapter 12). More of his work can be seen at www.catcherinthesky.net.

Photographs by Beryl Winifred Vivienne Ouimette who has been shooting photographs since she was twelve years old and has B.F.A. degrees in both graphic design and photography. Her address is berylwv@hotmail.com.

*To the memory of J. R. R. Tolkien for his intuitive understanding of
the dynamics underlying the horrors of the human past*

*To Philip Matthews for his undaunted hope for the human
future manifest through his outstanding contributions to interfaith
understanding and spiritual leadership*

Contents

PREFACE

On September 11th, an ancient scourge of the human species came out of hiding once again. The power of radical evil broke through our denial just as it did on December 7th, 1941.

What does this new escalation in violence and terror mean for us and for a prognosis of the human future? The increasing anxiety and chaos of our time have been fed by an arrogant and malignant secularist narcissism and nihilism that increasingly fosters arrogant fundamentalisms in response. At this time in history, it is imperative that we realize that both kinds of arrogance are being fueled by compulsive intrusions of archetypal energy tantamount to possession states.

J. R. R. Tolkien's *The Lord of the Rings* portrays a world in which a seductive and demonic lust for power over others grows in strength until it threatens to overwhelm the entire world. This fantasy masterpiece reflects an accurate intuition that such a process is active not in "Middle Earth" but on Planet Earth.

Working as both a Jungian psychoanalyst and spiritual theologian, my recent research has focused on the powerful, grandiose "god-energies" that burn fiercely in the heart of every human being. When we face these energies consciously in faith and with authentic respect, they reflect in us the numinous, creative, and transformative power of the divine presence. But when the human

ego engages in a pretentious "unknowing" of the reality and significance of this presence, the result is existential idolatry and
malignant narcissism.

Existential denial of the divine presence creates a demonic
alchemy that hijacks the sacred energies of the soul and twists
them into destructive powers of hideous strength, powers of
aggressive nonbeing that reveal themselves as addiction, racism,
sexism, homophobia, all forms of political oppression, ritual violence and war, and the ecological destruction of our planet. These
same grandiose energies fuel both corporate greed and religious
fundamentalism.

Carl Jung was the first modern psychological researcher to see
clearly the great dragon of grandiose energies lurking within us,
never sleeping but waiting for the light of our awareness to grow
dim before striking at the heart of humanity and civilization.
Traditional mythologies often used the mythic image of the dragon to indicate an intuition of these great and dangerous forces that
lurk within the human soul and turn satanic when left unconscious or treated with disrespect. Jung called us to face the reality
of these great energies and take moral and spiritual responsibility
for their conscious and creative incarnation in psyche and history.
In his *Answer to Job*, he accurately assessed our current situation in
the following terms:

> Everything now depends on man: immense power of
> destruction is given into his hand, and the question is
> whether he can resist the will to use it, and can temper his
> will with the spirit of love and wisdom. He will hardly be
> capable of doing so on his own unaided resources. He needs
> the help of an "advocate" in heaven. . . . The only thing that
> really matters now is whether man can climb up to a higher
> moral level, to a higher plane of consciousness, in order to be

equal to the superhuman powers which the fallen angels
have played into his hands. (quoted in Stein 1995, p. 168)

Never before has Jung's psychology and prophetic vision been so
timely or so urgently needed as now.

This book attempts to carry forward the work of Jung and also
the work of Edward Edinger in alerting us to the ways in which we
humans are vulnerable as never before to having our psyches
invaded and possessed by archetypal energies of great power. We
must all be vigilant to the insidious – usually unconscious – temptation to open the door to these forces within ourselves and act
them out in a demonic way. These psychic invasions and archetypal colonizations often coerce us into terrible acts of hate, violence, and inhumanity. We have seen what individuals possessed
by these grandiose archetypal forces are capable of.

Is there any antidote to this powerful lust for the "ring of
power"? I agree with Carl Jung and Paul Tillich that the antidote
is present, effective, and far more powerful than the toxins that
afflict us. Where is this antidote? It lies in increasing the light of
our spiritual and psychological awareness and respectful acceptance of the dragon within and the implications of its presence.

Both psychoanalytic research and spiritual theology have much
to teach us about the cause, dynamics, and cure of this cancer of
the soul. It is my hope that through an innovative partnership of
spiritual wisdom and psychoanalytic science we may be able to ini-
tiate a new and effective "Fellowship of the True Ring" and a new
kind of magi who, like Gandalf, do not retreat into despair in the
face of radical evil. These post-tribal twenty-first-century magi,
drawing upon a truly theonomous creative collaboration between
spirituality and science, will have the faith, wisdom, courage, and
skills to confront evil even more effectively than the tribal shamans
of old. Together they will seek to facilitate the incarnation in

history of what Tillich called the true "spiritual community."

This volume is the third in a series presenting newly edited versions of material I first delivered during the 1980s and early 1990s in lectures and other unpublished forums or in publications no longer readily available. These works share a common background in that they resulted from reflection on the kinds of situations that analysands in my psychoanalytic practice characteristically brought forward for treatment, personal situations commonly encountered in today's world that also relate directly to many of the most profound social problems in contemporary life.

The first volume in the series, *The Archetype of Initiation: Sacred Space, Ritual Process, and Personal Transformation* (2001), responds to the human need to surmount problem situations by entering "sacred space" with the help of a competent "ritual elder," first to reevaluate life and achieve transformation and then to return back to the ordinary world with renewed understanding and sense of purpose. Based on extensive field research and the work of such scholars as Arnold van Gennep, Mircea Eliade, Joseph Campbell, and Victor Turner, the book urges contemporary healers to utilize premodern tribal principles of sacred space and ritual process long considered lost or inaccessible to modern culture. The modern world's failure to understand these principles and prepare enough knowledgeable ritual elders has led to an epidemic of problems for which contemporary secular culture has no answer.

The second volume in the series, *The Magician and the Analyst: The Archetype of the Magus in Occult Spirituality and Jungian Analysis* (2002), makes available the original text of the pioneering research monograph entitled, "The Liminal and the Liminoid in Ritual Process and Analytical Practice," first presented in 1986 to the C. G. Jung Institute of Chicago. A new introductory essay describes the research journey that led to this rediscovery of transformational space.

This volume, *Facing the Dragon,* shows how pathological narcissism results from archetypal energies that are not contained and channeled through resources such as spiritual disciplines, ritual practice, utilization of the mythic imagination, and Jungian analysis. In the larger social sense, unconscious and uncontrolled grandiosity all too often leads well-intentioned groups into a malignant, pathological tribalism that wreaks havoc on their neighbors and threatens the rest of the world.

Chapters 1 and 12 present my current assessment of these issues as a continuing psychological and spiritual challenge. Chapters 2 through 8 and chapter 10 come from lectures and discussions held at the C. G. Jung Institute of Chicago. The edited text of these chapters retains some instances where audience members enriched the discussion by interjecting comments, raising questions, or asking for clarification. Chapter 9 comes from a paper presented at a symposium on "Jealousy, Envy, and Hatred Among the World's Religions." Chapter 11, "Dragon Laws," was specially written for this volume to provide a systematic outline of insights for confronting personal, social, and spiritual grandiosity. The chapter notes and bibliography include some updated references that have appeared in the intervening years.

The issues addressed here have significant implications for the future of human civilization on Planet Earth and must be faced by all of us. Not just religious leaders and psychotherapists but people from all areas and walks of life should look within themselves for evidence of these recurring phenomena and set themselves upon a path of increasing awareness. The problem, in other words, is not only "out there" but also always "in here" as well.

ACKNOWLEDGMENTS

As a child in the pre–Civil Rights era of the American South, I knew something was dreadfully wrong. Cruelty and hate were woven into the fabric of everyday life along with the massive denial characteristic of sentimentalist piety. For a time as a young man active in the Civil Rights movement, I entertained the popular fantasy that the malady was unique to southern culture. It took a long journey of study and experience to realize that it is an equal opportunity affliction present in all human psychology and spiritual life. I want to begin these acknowledgments with my parents, Golden Franklin Moore, Sr., and Margaret DePriest Moore. In my father's courageous stand as an educator against bigotry and bullies I saw that resistance to injustice was not only possible but a requirement for a mature man or woman. My mother, also an educator, offered a clear sense of orientation and priorities—"Son, seek first the Kingdom of Heaven." From her I learned about the existence of an authentic Transpersonal Center for life. They could not tell me how long it would take to find a basic "good enough" centeredness and integration in a psyche with roots in three cultures: Cajun Catholic, Russian Jewish, and Scotch-Irish Protestant. But their examples gave me strength for a long and continuing journey. They are always with me.

I often tell people that I needed Jung's concept of the collective unconscious to build bridges between the various tribes in my psyche. It took a long time to realize that the external human family needed Jung just as much as my internal one. Here I want to thank those who introduced me to the power of the thought of Carl Jung and, later, to his school of psychoanalysis. In Dallas in 1965, Frank Bockus, a young professor, showed me the size of Jung's vision and its potential for making partners of psychoanalysis and spirituality. Frank, I will always be in your debt. My subsequent mentors in Jungian thought and practice are too many to mention here, but I want to give special thanks to analysts June Singer and Lee Roloff, who represent for many of us outstanding examples of how to live the analytical life with grace and creativity.

I would also be remiss if I did not mention the many contributions of Texas analyst James Hall to both Jungian psychology and the dialogue between psychology and spirituality. To an aspiring young Jungian from the southwest his fine theoretical and clinical mind, along with his Stetson hat and cowboy boots, offered me a green light to pursue the analytical quest! Thank you, James.

The roots of this book are grounded in the work of the Institute for World Spirituality. In 1987, with the help of my wife, psychoanalyst Margaret Shanahan, and two outstanding scholar-writers, J. Gordon Melton and Douglas Gillette, I founded IWS to facilitate interfaith peace and reconciliation. Our vision was to utilize psychoanalytic resources, especially the concept of the collective unconscious, to facilitate meaningful dialogue between the various religious tribes of the human family. The Institute sponsored the Paulist Press series on Jungian Psychology and World Spiritual Traditions which Margaret and I continue to edit.

I especially want to acknowledge the steady and continuing friendship and support of my friend Phil Matthews and the Northern Star Foundation. Through his aid the Institute also pioneered in the facilitation of, not only high-level interfaith dialogues between serious spiritual practitioners, but also interfaith cooperative compassionate action in prison rehabilitation, microcredit initiatives for the world's poor, and research for a comprehensive encyclopedia and directory of all of the world's religious groups. The latter was envisioned as a major way to improve communication between the various spiritual tribes.

Here I want to thank all of the many people who contributed to the work of IWS between August 1987 and December 2000. Through your cooperative efforts you made a creative contribution to the cause of interfaith peace and reconciliation. I deeply regret that I could not find adequate financial resources to continue IWS and its work. In 2003, the need is even greater than it was in 2000, and I am more convinced than ever that the vision that began the work of IWS is correct and should be promoted as widely as possible. Because of limited financial resources, however, in December 2000, Project Return in New Orleans assumed leadership for the interfaith prison initiatives and the Council for the World Parliament of Religions assumed leadership for interfaith microcredit initiatives.

The Institute for the Study of American Religions has continued the research for the comprehensive database of the world's spiritual tribes. As I write this I have just received a copy of the first edition of the historic *Religions of the World: A Comprehensive Encyclopedia of Beliefs and Practices* (Melton and Baumann 2002). This most complete database on the spiritual communities of the world will continue to grow in the years to come. It will undoubtedly prove to be the most significant contribution of IWS to the challenge of interfaith communication and understanding.

Since 2001, the Institute for Psychoanalysis, Culture, and Spirituality has continued the work of applying psychoanalytic insight and research to the continuing challenge of the psychological, moral, and spiritual maturation of our species.

I would like to thank IPCS and the Northern Star Foundation for underwriting the costs of the preparation of the many drafts that were to become this book. Appreciation goes to Eva Salmons for careful transcription of my lectures. To Max Havlick, my gifted editor at New World Community Enterprises, goes the credit for bringing a variety of materials from lectures and seminars into a coherent, integrated, and understandable manuscript. The remaining awkwardness of my efforts at prose is solely my responsibility. With Robert Bly and John Lee encouraging me, I hope to improve my writing in the next decade!

I also want to thank Murray Stein and Siobhan Drummond of Chiron Publications for their interest in this book and their willingness to aid me in bringing these reflections to a public struggling to make sense of the current epidemic of interreligious hatred and violence.

Finally, I want to thank my wife Margaret, who continues to be an exciting and challenging partner in exploring the many and fascinating ways in which Jung's psychology aids us all in opening to a larger, more loving, and radiantly human life.

—*Robert Moore*

The Big Smile

CHAPTER I

The Lucifer Complex and the Enemy Within

Psychological Reflections on Human Evil

T HOMAS BRUNNER (2000) RECENTLY COMPARED MY work with that of Thomas Moore and characterized it as follows: "While Thomas Moore's books may be sifted down into the maxim, 'the sacred is closer than you think,' Robert Moore's books exhibit the central idea that 'the demonic is closer than you think.'" This distinction misses some of the subtleties of my understanding of the important connection between the sacred and evil, but it does accurately characterize the urgency of my concern that we as individuals, groups, political and cultural tribes, and as a species, quickly come to a more adequate dynamic understanding of the great solar fires that operate unconsciously within us to drive the increasing epidemics of personal and social evil.

Why do I emphasize the dynamics of human evil in my research and teaching in psychology and spirituality?[1] Because any approach to spirituality that hopes to confront the personal and communal destructiveness threatening the human future must avoid several traps. First, we must avoid the New Age tendency to deny the reality and power of evil. This widespread "flight into the light" is particularly tempting today because it requires so little in the way of either reflection or action. It enables continued denial of the seriousness of the situation, and denial of how we as individuals participate in our own destruction, and the destruction of our communities and planet.

Second, we must avoid the historically popular tendency to find a human "other" to serve as a scapegoat for explanation of the impact of evil in our lives, one who can serve as a receptacle for our shadow projections, and who, if they are imprisoned, tortured, burned, bombed, and so forth, can be used as ritual sacrificial victims to give us a bogus sense of mastery over our desperate situation. These misguided strategies were ably discussed by Ernest Becker in *Escape from Evil* (1985) and *The Denial of Death* (1975). Racism, classism, anti-Semitism, religious bigotry, and other misguided tribalisms have majored in this seductive but demonic attempt to locate and suppress or destroy the "toxins" that afflict us.

Sexism has been a historic and even more ubiquitous strategy for finding a scapegoat. Both men and women must share the responsibility for starting to break the historic pattern of blaming the other gender for human destructiveness and evil. As some feminist theorists have pointed out, the different genders may experience different patterns of temptation or vulnerability to various forms of sin or evil, but neither one should continue to explain evil by reference to gender. Both genders and persons of all classes, races, religions, and sexual preferences participate in the experience of evil, and all are responsible for its perpetuation. All must respond to the challenge of coming to an understanding of evil that is neither naïve nor grounded in scapegoating of the other, but which may account for some of the forces of destructiveness that threaten to destroy us.

WHAT ARE THE MARKS OF HUMAN EVIL?

Being able to talk with any authority about evil is not one of the strengths of modern "flatland" secular culture. Take, for example, the case of the Holocaust. Witness how difficult we have found it to face our tendency to split off our consciousness of the Holocaust, to avoid looking at it, to let our denial of the reality and power of its evil overwhelm us either by minimizing or trivializing the significance of the war against the Jews. Responses range from absolving the Germans of their responsibility for the Holocaust to forcing the German people to carry the collective shadow for the whole human species. We hate to admit the fact that the genocidal impulse is species-wide. Even Hannah Arendt's emphasis on the "banality of evil" in the Holocaust experience has made it easier for us to engage in massive denial of the power and pervasiveness of radical evil in human experience.

Modern theologians have, for the most part, been little help. Recent theology tends to discuss *theodicy:* Can God be a good God, given the manifest evil in the world? Long discussions usually focus on the nature and limits of the power of God, and whether or not God wills evil or merely permits it, willingly or unwillingly. Thousands of pages elucidate the various perspectives one might take on such issues. Scholars with a philosophical bent may find some of these discussions interesting and provocative, but they tend not to be, as we say today, "experience near." They seem rather to treat evil as if it were merely an interesting academic issue for discussion in graduate-level seminars.

This is a classic way of responding to evil by those who have not achieved an adequate warrior initiation.[2] Contemporary philosophers and theologians differ from the shamans of tribal culture in their lack of maturation in the warrior line of psychological and spiritual development. In contrast to our modern clergy and psy-

chotherapists, not to speak of our professors, the great tribal
shamans knew that their roles as healers and spiritual leaders
required them to be warriors as well. Tribal peoples also treated
these issues in a sophisticated way in their mythologies. While we
obviously need to get beyond the limitations of tribal perspectives,
we also need to ask if there is not significant wisdom for us in the
ancient narrative traditions about evil.

Tribal peoples saw careful thinking about the nature and
dynamics of evil as a serious practical matter central to personal and
communal existence and critical to the survival of the human community. I do not share the view of many scholars today who ascribe
this interest to primitive superstition or to the effects of sociopolitical structures of domination. Contemporary "scholarly" dismissals
of premodern tribal wisdom on these issues are as arrogant,
grandiose, and inflated as they are ubiquitous. Contemporary theologians are, for the most part, no more appreciative of these traditions from folklore and mythology than the secular, reductionistic
social and behavioral scientists. Long before a few contemporary
theologians began to rediscover the centrality of mythic narratives
in articulating spiritual truth, tribal peoples had spent thousands of
years perfecting mythic narrative and storytelling as ways to provide
in-depth understanding of the nature and dynamics of the human
experience of evil.[3] I agree with Carl Jung that we must return to
mine this ancient wisdom of the human mythic imagination if we
are to regain an adequate capacity to discern and confront the presence and power of human evil today.

EVIL IN FOLKLORE AND MYTHOLOGY

From an extensive comparative study of ancient wisdom traditions
I have distilled the following list of assumptions they held about

the nature and dynamics of evil:

1. Evil is a reality with an agency of its own.

2. The presence of evil can be felt in the enchanting power of denial on individual, familial, cultural levels, the seductive power of what the philosopher and theologian Paul Tillich called "dreaming innocence."

3. The chief tactic of evil is to present the human individual and community with a false, deceptive representation of reality. In short, it lies.

4. Evil, therefore, has the capacity to clothe and disguise itself in forms that seem innocent, good, or at least justified, and have a seductive attractiveness.

5. Being near this evil enchantment causes you to lose your powers of discernment and vigilance, and your spiritual and moral light grows dim. Its influence is contagious. Tribal peoples around the world recognized this danger and built elaborate systems of taboo and ritual "insulation" against it.

6. An evil presence can get inside your community, family, home, and body, and even into your psyche, before you realize the danger exists. It is already "in the house" by the time you realize you have a problem.

7. Once inside, evil begins to erode the foundations of personal and social life by presenting itself as the true center of life. It functions as a "black hole," a powerful vortex that, in effect, attacks Being itself. This is the human reality behind the biblical injunction against idolatry, "You shall have no other gods before me." We can read it this way, "You shall not create bogus or pseudocenters for your life and society."

8. Evil multiplies itself on your energy, your lifeblood, your creativity. It co-opts your good and often magnificent energies and potentials, and makes them serve hatred, sadism, oppression,

and the destruction of health and life. It recruits and diverts the energies of life and creativity into the service of death.

9. Evil denies the reality of death and all human limitations. It makes an insatiable, limitless quest the substitute for legitimate expansion of the individual self. It puts polymorphous desires and pleasures in place of a social concern for community and the consequences of one's actions. It infects us with what Kierkegaard called "the sickness of infinitude."

10. The presence of evil can be seen in its effects on the persons and community around it. It is not simply an idea or an absence of some positive quality. It is an active, aggressive, antilife force that attacks the health and vitality of everyone around it. "You shall know them by their fruits."

These insights caused many cultures to describe the phenomenology of evil with mythic images of a vampire that thrives on the absence of light (see Shanahan 1994). You are most vulnerable to it when you are the most disconnected from your relationships and trying to cope with your life and problems alone. It manifests great intelligence, as if it has lived many lifetimes and has methodically developed a capacity to detect and exploit personal weaknesses and blind spots. It preys in a seductive way on your rightful need for attention and recognition that is not in itself demonic. It captures your love and turns it into necrophilia. It captures your legitimate assertiveness and turns it into sadism. It captures your knowledge and uses it for deception, greed, and antisocial manipulation. It captures your desire to nurture and turns it into domination and oppression.

In contemporary culture, even when many theologians have become lost in their own enchanted "innocence," the intuitive understanding of evil expresses itself in an extraordinary way in such movies as *Invasion of the Body Snatchers, The Exorcist, Cape*

Fear, the Alien series, *Looking for Mr. Goodbar, The Andromeda Strain, Silkwood,* and many others.

Consider, for example, the recent remake by John Carpenter of the science fiction classic *The Thing* (1982), starring Kurt Russell. In an isolated arctic outpost some scientists discover a space ship in the ice. The wreck has been buried there for centuries. Lying dormant in the wreckage is an alien creature with the capacity to change forms, invade, and attach in a parasitical way to other life forms to increase its size and strength while destroying the individuality of those life forms it co-opts and colonizes. The first group of scientists to discover the wreckage are naïve about the potential risks to themselves and do not take proper precautions. Their research colony is "contaminated" by the alien and, though they fight back, all except one man are killed by the alien.

When the movie begins, we see a dog approaching our camp, being chased across the tundra and fired upon by a man in a helicopter. The dog runs into the camp and mixes with our dogs. The man in the helicopter lands, shouts in a seemingly berserk way, and continues to fire at the dog until others respond by shooting and killing him. Only much later do we learn that the alien had infected the dog and the man was trying to kill the dog to prevent the infection from spreading. People did not understand his mission, so he was killed instead.

As the movie progresses, one individual after another is contaminated by contagion with "the thing," and their naiveté about its presence makes it impossible for them to protect themselves. The shaman-warrior consciousness finally manifests in Kurt Russell's character who does the investigation necessary to discover the reality of the radical danger posed by the intruder. He is horrified to find that the alien is already in the camp and has found a way to invade the human body without being seen. Only a blood testing by fire can determine the presence of the infection.

As the contagion in the camp spreads, the various sources of heat and light are gradually destroyed. The shamanic warrior figure realizes that "the thing" must be contained at any cost, including his own life. At the end of the movie he faces the horror of "the thing" with only his steely resolve and fire as a weapon. The audience gets a sense of the incredible magnitude of the power and malignant agency of the power of evil that infected the human community. Though we are shaken by the power, resourcefulness, and focused intentionality of the demonic presence, we still admire the valiant courage of the human response once the radical nature of the situation was discerned.

While the movie picks up the ancient themes of invasion and contagion by evil, its ending reflects the contemporary tendency toward hopelessness about the power of evil. This probably explains why we prefer to deny evil rather than to face it, because we see little possibility of overcoming it.

This underscores my point that folklore and mythology contain the deepest, wisest, and most sustained reflections we have on evil and what to do about it. In contrast to recent, more shallow understandings of evil as merely a willful choosing to act destructively, tribal cultures were clear about the radical reality, power, and ego-alien agency of evil. They had a deep sense of evil as possession, as having a cause or agency beyond the conscious ego, one that seduces individuals into states of enchantment that compromise their ability to liberate themselves or even realize the destructiveness of their behavior.

Even more importantly, the myths of tribal cultures also saw the human potential for discerning, understanding, confronting, and liberating the human community from possession by evil. Liberation, usually seen as a form of exorcism, required consultation with the shaman or sorcerer and an appeal to the concern and action of the wider community. Powers beyond the individual person and family had to be brought to bear on the toxic, enchanting influences until the individual could be restored to normal human functioning.

In short, traditional societies spent far more time trying to understand and combat evil than does contemporary society. Modern culture has managed to make itself so blind to the reality of evil that it has become almost incapable of discerning the magnitude of its threat to the human future. How else can we explain the pervasive denial of evil that dominates our time? By turning away from the resources of the mythic imagination, we have stripped ourselves of the capacity to cut through our denial of the destructive forces that we face.

RESOURCES FROM PSYCHOANALYTIC REFLECTION

But wait, are we not simply romanticizing and mystifying tribal cultures? Is there any contemporary evidence to support the idea that the engines of radical evil come from outside the human ego, that evil is really a possession and enchantment of the human self, and not simply a misguided conscious act of an otherwise perfectly rational and intact human ego? Has psychoanalysis, for instance, discovered anything remotely resembling the traditional views of evil?

Viewed cross-culturally, the traditional views support the existence of what we might call a "Lucifer complex" that threatens to seduce and possess the human ego consciousness. In some cultures, this toxic alien presence is conceptualized as demons, in others as idolatry, in others as the power of the temptations of illusion and desire. This presence usually promises both significance and satisfaction of desire, the eclipse of limitations, and the ability to become the center of the world. Its final outcome

is almost universally recognized as hubris, madness, and a resulting destruction of the human community and human life.

Several different schools of psychoanalysis have indeed provided concepts and compelling clinical evidence for reappropri-
ating the traditional views of evil with renewed respect and
appreciation. Not only have they discovered evidence of such a
reality, but they have provided unprecedented revolutionary ways
to understand the widespread nature of this phenomenon in
human life, that it is not only a tribal reality, but a human,
species-wide one.

Contemporary psychoanalytic studies of the nature and
dynamics of narcissism relate directly to traditional understandings of the dynamics of human evil. Heinz Kohut and the psychoanalytic self psychologists were not the first to discover the destructive results of pathological infantile grandiosity. A careful scrutiny
of various schools of psychoanalytic psychology reveals general
belief in the presence in the human psyche of what I call the
"Great Self Within," a very real inner presence that is not the same
as a healthy human self or ego, but can take possession of an ego
and drive it to fragmentation and total destruction.[4] This "Great
Self Within," also called the god-complex or the god-imago, has
sometimes been equated with Satan or the devil, but it is much
more complex than the imago of Satan. It is not evil in itself, even
though it does fuel the Luciferian tendency.

Later chapters will discuss how unconscious identification
with this inner reality can lead both into possession states and
splitting of the human psyche. Here we will tour the history of
psychoanalysis for clues to the reality of the "Great Self Within."
Depth psychologists from Freud to Kohut observed a tendency
for the human ego to be overwhelmed by "grandiose," godlike
claims grounded in psychological systems beyond the awareness
of the ego.

Freud on the Id and Superego. In the classical psychoanalysis of Sigmund Freud, the "Great Self Within" was not perceived with the clarity about its structural cohesiveness that is possible today. Nevertheless, Freud did note and posit structures in the unconscious that manifest phenomena that I believe are generated by the same reality. Freud's structural theory described two powerful inner realities that manifested godlike claims in different ways: the id and the superego. The id (the it) was the driving force behind totalistic instinctual drives for sex and aggression, the insatiable appetites of the pleasure principle and archaic desire.[5] One could say that the appetites of the id are larger than human, godlike in their totalistic and grandiose claims. The archaic superego, on the other hand, is not grandiose in its desire for instinctual discharge but in its total, perfectionist demand for compliance with the highest ideals and standards.

Although Freud did not conceptualize these two systems together as comprising a "Great Self Within," he did describe phenomena reflecting something within the self that makes grandiose, godlike claims on the individual, often leading to illness and worse if not properly confronted and regulated. Freud, therefore, was the first scientific psychological researcher to identify powerful grandiose forces in the psyche that the conscious ego must learn to recognize and relate to in a positive and effective way if life is to be served.

Alfred Adler on the Superiority Complex. Alfred Adler's thought highlights the reality of the "Great Self Within" more clearly than does Freud's. In Adler's view, all psychopathology, including the experience of the "inferiority complex," results from a usually hidden "superiority complex" that is not available to the consciousness of the individual. This unacknowledged claim to superiority leads the individual to feel entitled and exempt from the limits and claims of human existence, and subsequently to engage in a variety of dysfunctional and abusive behaviors. While Adler was more of a phenomenological psychologist who did not emphasize deep structures in the psyche, it is striking that he founded his theories on the idea that human destructiveness results from an unacknowledged unconscious psychological orientation with an antisocial claim to superiority, and that a psychological cure requires disidentification from this grandiose attitude.

Carl Jung on the Archetypal Self. Carl Jung has given us the clearest delineation of the "Great Self Within." Jung not only affirmed the existence of such an archetypal Self beyond the ego, but unlike many of his more naïve and romantic followers, he warned us to take great care lest this archetypal self overwhelm the ego with its grandiose energies.

We must carefully distinguish Jung's position on this issue from those of some of his successors. Many who call themselves "archetypal psychologists" do not retain Jung's concept of the archetypal Self but represent a so-called "deconstructionist" position in psychology. Even though they focus on images and the imagination, they do not offer a coherent theory of psychological deep structures that ground the imagination, or articulate an understanding of any transegoic great Self rooted in the collective unconscious.

My own research has convinced me that Jung was correct in his formulations, and that he can help us understand how the engines of human evil are grounded in the reality and power of an archetypal "Great Self Within." How, then, does this inner reality relate to evil? Cultures around the world taught that the great engine of evil was arrogance, or hubris, as the Greeks called it. Tribal cultures often thought that the movement into arrogance resulted from possession by a god or demon. Psychoanalytic research has helped us understand how deeply insightful these early cultures were, but it has also helped us go beyond them in understanding the results of possession by these grandiose energies. We now know that the psyche splits and cannot maintain its structural integrity when it cannot relate to these "divine energies" in a conscious and constructive way.

FACING THE DRAGON

Throughout human history, spiritual masters and sages have utilized various mythological images to symbolize the presence and power of the grandiose energies they intuited to be present in the depths of the human psyche. My own research has found no mythic image for these energies used more often than that of the dragon. World mythology presents the dragon with two different faces: the dragon as enemy, and the dragon as a source of power and blessing.

Western spiritual traditions have tended to emphasize the interpretation of the "dragon as enemy," the nemesis of human life, a tradition best exemplified by the classic *Beowulf* (see Heaney 2000 and Rauer 2000). The task was to slay the great beast, called by many names, including Behemoth and Leviathan. Human life and civilization somehow depended on the success of the dragon-slayer.

The other tradition is more characteristic of Eastern spiritual traditions, both Christian and non-Christian. Here the dragon, including the "Great Self Within," is not demonized, but seen rather as a beneficent resource to be related to consciously for its transformative, regenerative energies.

The lectures presented in the following chapters address the human concerns reflected in the Beowulf traditions: the necessity for vigilance in discerning the dragon's presence, and the dragon's threat to personal, social, and spiritual life when one encounters it unprepared. Lack of a sophisticated consciousness of the dragon within leaves us defenseless against the evil effects of its invasion into our personal and social lives. Any realistic hope for a promising personal or planetary future requires us, like Beowulf, to wake up and face the dragon of personal and spiritual grandiosity.

NOTES

1. For over two decades I have taught graduate seminars on the dynamics of the sacred and the dynamics of evil and the relationships between them. See my lectures on psychology and evil available from the C. G. Jung Institute of Chicago.
2. The processes of initiation have been a constant theme of my work for many years. See my recent collection of lectures and essays (Moore 2001).
3. Mythology and folklore abound in references to evil, its nature and dynamics. See especially Forsythe (1987) and von Franz (1974).
4. For my decoding of the inner structure and dynamics of these inner realities, see my lectures on "The Great Self Within," available through the bookstore of the C. G. Jung Institute of Chicago. Order information appears on my website at www.robertmoore-phd.com.
5. Freud, then, was the modern researcher who rediscovered the horrific reality of "the thing."

CHAPTER 2

The Archetype of Spiritual Warfare

This longing to commit a madness stays with us throughout our lives. Who has not, when standing with someone by an abyss or high up on a tower, had a sudden impulse to push the other over? And how is it that we hurt those we love although we know that remorse will follow? Our whole being is nothing but a fight against the dark forces within ourselves.

To live is to war with trolls in heart and soul. To write is to sit in judgment on oneself.

—Henrik Ibsen

WHEN WE COME FACE TO FACE WITH EVIL, WE ENTER the territory of spiritual warfare, one of the most powerful archetypal themes in human history. After a few words about my own interest in the topic, this discussion reviews some images from various religious traditions, and then considers the psychodynamics of various aspects of spiritual warfare.[1]

Both as a psychoanalyst and as a professor of psychology and spirituality at the Chicago Theological Seminary, my chief concerns are psychology and religion as resources for the processes of human health and healing. Throughout my career I have studied the history of religions and comparative philosophy, ancient and modern. In what I call my proto-maturity, I became a Jungian, not because I knew nothing else, but because I decided that the

Jungian point of view was the most adequate psychology of the human available. I am more sure of that today than ever.

It is not that Jungians do not appreciate other points of view, because they are unique in how they appreciate other psychological schools and traditions and make places for them in their work. In today's cultural and planetary context, the Jungian point of view is, in my judgment, the only point of view with the comprehensive scope and complexity to address the problems of being human in a pan-tribal, postmodern way. Jungian thought has excellent resources for a truly human spirituality and a species-inclusive approach to both the psyche and human community. To be quite frank, the Jungian way of thinking about both personal and social issues is one of the few resources available today that holds much promise for a way out of the current frightening political, cultural, and planetary situation, a situation fueled by lack of awareness of the archetypal dynamics we work with in this discussion.

Therefore, although I am myself a professor, I do not consider this topic to have merely academic interest. It has great importance to us for many reasons. One, by no means the least important, is that only by studying this archetype of spiritual warfare can we really understand the power of the human penchant toward war and the spiritual and ethical implications of that instinct, and I do mean "instinct." This is important for us on the sociopolitical level, and we want to look at it in some depth.

Once you start trying to face and cope with the dragon energies in your life, you must take seriously the archetype of spiritual warfare and the psychological resources around it. If you do not have some sense of the warfare going on inside you at the psychological level, then you will be less able to do what you need to do to free yourself from the things trying to drag you down and imprison you and stifle your life. So a study of the archetype of spiritual warfare is important on both social and personal levels.

We will think about this spiritual warfare in the context of the Jungian understanding of the shadow side of human personality. We often talk about the "shadow" as a factor in the development of the individual psyche, but this discussion considers something else as well, the relationship between the personal shadow and the archetypal shadow.

RELIGIOUS TRADITIONS

We begin with an examination of the religion of the magi. Zoroastrianism is one of the most interesting and least studied topics in the field of history of religions. Even the best departments of religion rarely have a course on Zoroastrianism, and yet it is one of the most influential traditions, and it is still alive today. It is a living tradition. When I was in India last summer, the Parsis, as they call the Zoroastrians in India, were very active. Their Towers of Silence, where they expose their dead to the vultures to be cleansed, as they put it, are a prominent feature of the landscape in some of the major Indian cities.

To get at how some of these traditions interact, you may have heard that Zoroastrianism influenced Judaism, the Dead Sea Scrolls, and early Christianity, particularly in its imaging of a great apocalyptic warfare between two beings. Whether you call them both gods or not is a matter of interpretation, but in the Zoroastrian tradition, the divine reality is made up of two beings, one good and the other evil. The good god is Ahura Mazda, a name derived from words that have to do with light. The opposition is Ahriman. Different Zoroastrian traditions differ on the ultimate outcome of the cosmic struggle.

Zoroastrianism has a battle occurring at all times between Ahura Mazda, the god of light, and Ahriman, who is either a god of evil and darkness, or a very powerful demon, or *daeva*. Some traditions put them practically equal in power and suggest that the evil god is never defeated, that the struggle goes on and on forever. Other traditions suggest that at the end of time, Ahura Mazda will defeat Ahriman, and the war will end with good and light triumphing over evil and darkness. You can see how Judeo-Christian messianic reflection relates to this.

The Zoroastrians have this immense struggle. They capture what many later Christians and Jews lost, a sense of the spiritual struggle, or spirituality as a struggle. In studying spirituality today, you find many so-called spiritual masters selling themselves as peace-oriented gurus. Not *world* peace-oriented, but the kind of peace that says to meditate and get mellow. This kind of peace has no sense of the enormity of the human spiritual struggle. It misleads people, because it is fundamentally an enormous denial of what it takes to individuate.

Jung knew better. His emphasis was more like this: "You do not want to struggle? Then do not start toward individuation, because it will be all you can deal with and more to work toward your individuation." If you are not willing to struggle, it is best that you just allow a regressive restoration of your persona, and just take your medication and forget it, because struggle is the reality.

Audience: Some conservative and fundamentalist Christian groups, and some that might be classified as sects, have more of the idea of a spiritual battle where evil is a real power.

Moore: Exactly! That is one of their strengths, because anyone who is not overwhelmed with massive denial knows that it is a struggle. Human beings who are awake and dealing with their lives with fairly non-rose-colored glasses know that people are involved in an enormous struggle. They may not have a good education or a sophisticated psychological point of view, but when someone comes to them with images that capture the struggle of human experience, it is very attractive to them and speaks to their authentic experience.

That is why Islam is so powerful today, because it is based on the concept of *jihad* (Arabic for "effort" or "strife"). The problem with it is the same problem that fundamentalist Christians have, the phenomenon of splitting. The more primitive and borderline you are emotionally and developmentally, the more you will tend to split apart segments of your inner life, which means that you will tend to locate more of your enemy outside yourself and say, "You out there are my problem. If it were not for you, I would not have any problems."

In all fundamentalisms in all religions, the more fundamentalist you are, the more you engage in this psychological mechanism called splitting which means, "I am good, and you are bad. We are the people of God, and you are the people of Satan. We are the faithful, and you are the heathen." Splitting creates a crusade mentality. The demonic thing about the Crusades was that the Muslims operated out of the same kind of immature, regressive operation of this archetypal configuration as the Christians did. So you had these wonderful, courageous Muslim knights fighting these wonderful, courageous Christian knights, killing each other, all under the same archetypal configuration.

Audience: Do you think that this evaluation of a religion where people split things would bear out in psychological testing of individuals in the group? You seem to be describing something different from the way those groups would describe it, but what if you tested them on an individual level?

Moore: That is a good question for empirical scientific research. I would hypothesize that you will find more people who would diagnose as borderline personalities in high-intensity fundamentalist groups than in other religious bodies that use a more subtle diagnostics. Statistically, however, it would not be one-to-one, because this splitting phenomenon also occurs among radical liberals. It's just a question of who gets the demon projection. Ronald Reagan and the conservatives carry it for the left, and the liberals carry it for the fundamentalists. So in terms of psychological diagnostics, and spiritual hermeneutics as well, you have to look for how often people locate their enemy outside their own group.

This is not to doubt that real human enemies really do exist "out there," but the enemy is also "in here," inside each person. To the extent that you refuse to acknowledge the enemy within you, then emotionally you must project it somewhere else. In Jungian terms, you refuse to admit, "Yes, I have a shadow, and it is part of my problem, and it is part of your problem, and I am trying to deal with it the best I can." One of the borderline dynamics that results is that you have to expel your badness onto someone else. You can do a whole psychology of religious tribalism by looking at people who deny the badness within themselves and try to put it all out there on other people. That is one of the key dynamics in how the archetype of spiritual warfare operates.

It is not enough, however, to say like some Jungians that the evil is all inside, and any trouble I have with you is just because I have it in my shadow. "If I could just integrate my shadow then I would see you for the wonderful, complete, perfect person that you are." That is not true either. Such a position taken to extreme would suggest that if the Jews had just integrated their shadows in the late thirties, then Adolf Hitler would have seemed like a nice fellow. That can't be right. No matter how much the people in the ghettoes integrated their Jewish shadows, Hitler was still an objective reality out there in the real world trying to kill them. Remember the old joke, "Just because you are paranoid does not mean they are *not* out to get you." That is true in psychology as well.

Audience: Some groups like EST and Silva Mind Control seem

to say, "It is all in your attitude," but they don't seem to consider the reality of things like starvation in Ethiopia.

Moore: That is right. That is an exact example: the whole idea that all the world's problems are just in you. That is not true, of course. All the world's problems are not just in you. The idea that my problems are big enough to cause all the world's problems shows a rampant grandiosity. We all have our own grandiose fantasies of omnipotence, but that one is ridiculous!

The Zoroastrian tradition approaches what philosophy calls dualism: two beings, one of light and goodness, and one of darkness and evil. When you study world traditions it is amazing the extent to which you find this concept imaged everywhere throughout history and all over the world. Some traditions do not make the opposition into a full-fledged god, but they might portray it as a great dragon or a very powerful demon.

In Judaism and many other traditions, there is less emphasis on a godlike evil adversary. The Hebrew scriptures present Yahweh trying to bring about good and righteousness on earth, while the people Israel are often not righteous, not faithful to Yahweh, and not keeping their side of the covenant, thus failing in their mission. At the same time, the Canaanites also do many unrighteous things in Yahweh's eyes, but the Old Testament traditions do not lift them up to the status of a divine adversary transcendently grounded in some sort of metaphysical evil reality.

Nonetheless, the Hebrew tradition does give you a sense of the religious life as spiritual warfare. The whole idea of taking the land of Israel from its previous occupants is associated with Yahweh God leading his magnificent earthly warrior generals like Moses, Joshua, Deborah, and David. The war is sometimes against the mythic evil enemies Leviathan or Behemoth.

To understand how the archetype of spiritual warfare works in Judaism, you have to start with David and see his importance to

Jewish spirituality. David is the archetypal warrior general leading the armies of Israel into battle against the enemies of Israel. The early image of David fighting Goliath, for instance, shows spiritual warfare at its most archetypal, where the little hero encounters a large evil creature, but wins because he carries a divine blessing.

Many other traditions have this same motif of a hero fighting an archetypal battle against evil. The heroes may not be as strong as their evil opponents, but with a right heart, they can get assistance even from animals and seemingly chance encounters that give them a critical edge for pulling out a victory at the end.

Some scholars think the word *Pharisee* relates to the word *Parsi,* which refers to the Persian Zoroastrians who fled to India in the eighth century to escape persecution. This evidence may indicate Zoroastrian influence on traditions associated with the Pharisees.

The Dead Sea Scrolls also may show Zoroastrian influence during the intertestamental period, for their great theme is spiritual warfare. This small sectarian group of Jews believed in a great spiritual battle. They believed they knew where the battle was going to happen, that their own Teacher of Righteousness would lead them in the battle, and that they would receive the materials they needed to win a great victory over the forces of darkness. They were not Christians, but some scholars see similarities between their community and the early Christian communities that taught about Jesus. The idea of a Teacher of Righteousness who would come and lead the community to victory in a great final battle seems very close to the formative imagery in some early Christian writings that would emerge a few years later.

This material is now available in paperback, *The Dead Sea Scriptures,* edited by Theodor Gaster (1964). The selections are very readable and straightforward, and many of them are ancient texts unknown before the 1950s. Many of them were preserved in good condition, and there may be others out there in the hills outside Jerusalem. A shepherd found them in jars inside a cave. The material in them is amazing. The beauty of it for our purposes is that you can read this apocalyptic imagery in uncorrupted, unadulterated form: "This is the final battle. The enemy forces are coming in over there. We have to get organized this way. Our Teacher of Righteousness will be our general." It lays out the organization of the troops and all that sort of thing. It is amazing apocalyptic material.[2]

Audience: It sounds like the people who get out their charts and maps and talk about the Battle of Armageddon. A lot of fundamentalist preachers talk about a second coming of Christ when he will come back with a great sword and win a great victory over evil.

Moore: Yes, it is similar. They come out of the same tradition. There is an archetypal configuration behind all that kind of thinking. The archetype of spiritual warfare deals with apocalyptic images of final warfare. Armageddon is one of the images that came early from that tradition.

Audience: You mention dualistic traditions but then two divine realities. As one trained in philosophy, I can think in terms of a real split between two realities, like mind and body, or spirit and body, but not between two *divine* realities, because that puts spirit out there, for example, and evil in here, and isn't that splitting too? Isn't that where a lot of problems come into Christianity?

Moore: That is the Manichean view that came out of this splitting. Some traditions make the two opposing forces two different gods, while other traditions make one of them God, and one of them Satan, as in some Christian traditions.

What does Christianity teach about Lucifer? In the myths, Lucifer was the highest ranked of all the angels. The best literature on that is the four-volume set on the cultural and intellectual history of the concept of Satan by Jeffery Burton Russell, a historian at the University of California, and he just happens to appreciate Jungian thought too. That is an extra bonus. The first volume is *The Devil: Perceptions of Evil from Antiquity to Primitive Christianity* (1977); the second volume is *Satan: The Early Christian Tradition* (1981); the third is *Lucifer: The Devil in the Middle Ages* (1984); and the fourth is called *Mephistopheles: The Devil in the Modern World* (1986). Cornell University Press published all four volumes, so you can trace the idea of opposition to God from the beginning of the Judeo-Christian tradition right up to the present.

You learn from Russell's work that the history of Christian tradition has a lot more in it about spiritual warfare than you hear in modern churches. You can find it in *The City of God* by Augustine (354–430), which lays it all out: "There was a rebellion, and Lucifer took with him a whole wing of the divine forces that were loyal to him" (Augustine 1950). This medieval hierarchy of angels is not taught in most seminaries today, not even Catholic seminaries. You can become a Catholic priest today without knowing much about the old medieval hierarchy of angels.

The medieval writings show a hierarchy at work in the rebellion, just like the movie *Star Wars* (1977, written and directed by George Lucas). Each of the two groups of forces has a counterpart from the top down. Throughout the medieval angelology you had this kind of layout of spiritual warfare. In both these earlier Christian traditions and Islam, each person has an assigned demon. We all know the folk tradition that everyone has an angel looking out for them, but did you know that you also have your own personal demon assigned to you?

C. S. Lewis did a similar thing in *The Screwtape Letters* (1942). You have a demon assigned to you to see if he can disrupt your life, and you also have an angel of life assigned to try to foil the demon. In our popular culture, the comedian Flip Wilson has a routine centered on "the devil made me do it." We also have popular cartoon art that shows a little devil and a little angel whispering to the main character to get them to do something. We joke about it, but it was no joke in these traditions. They were serious about it.

Audience: For the apostle Paul in his writings certainly, it was a matter of "powers and principalities," and spiritual powers always in contention, and of Christians putting on spiritual armor.

Moore: The "full armor of God" and "the breastplate of righteousness" (see Ephesians 6:10–17). Paul's letters present many images like this in martial terms. Without some historical and contextual background, you would not have the slightest idea what Paul meant by "principalities and powers," that the apocalyptic struggle involves trans-human forces. Spiritual warfare, in other words, would still be going on in the universe even if there were no human beings in it at all. It is cosmic and occurs at all levels.

Audience: Madeleine L'Engle in her Time Quartet books deals with that.

Moore: Tell us about her. Does she write science fiction, or fantasy fiction?

Audience: She is hard to classify. Madeleine L'Engle was an artist-in-residence at St. John the Divine Cathedral in New York, and she wrote books that are like kid's books, but publishers wouldn't take them for a long time because they seemed too much like science fiction or fantasy. It didn't quite fit their categories. It was too advanced for kids, and too adolescent for adults. She has one group fighting with cosmic powers on behalf of good, while the other group, the Echthroids, are evil powers threatening to undo creation.[3]

Moore: Fantasy fiction and science fiction are the only places you get a powerful representation of this idea today, other than in fundamentalist religious forms like the Islamic radicals or the Christian right.

Audience: And in Saturday morning cartoons.

Moore: That's right. You have it clearly represented there. I also think of how Tolkien and C. S. Lewis dealt with spiritual warfare while writing from an archetypal apocalyptic perspective. There is a lot of literary criticism about this kind of Christian heroic fiction.[4]

GNOSTICISM

Audience: Does Gnosticism fall into this group?

Moore: Gnosticism in some ways is similar to Manicheanism, but it is not one phenomenon. Gnosticism is a complicated topic. It is based on the idea that there is an esoteric knowledge not shared by everyone. This esoteric knowledge reveals the nature and content of the struggle going on in the world, and what is required to deal with it. The term *gnosis* (Greek, "knowledge") means possession of special revealed knowledge needed for your salvation or transformation. The uninitiated, by contrast, walk around without the knowledge they need to know about what is really going on in the world. Paul's writings have a similar idea, because he talks about starting you off with a small amount of elementary knowledge, but not the mature food. "You are babes now, but when you are ready, I can give you more solid food that amounts to advanced mystical understanding, and then you will be able to see what this is all about."[5]

The orthodox Christian tradition declared Gnosticism a heresy largely because it made the body and the world evil, and that is a heresy. Orthodox theology considers Jesus both fully divine and fully human, which means he really had a body and he really died. Gnostics tried to say, "No, he didn't really have a body, or if he had a body, then he didn't really die." That comes from the Manichean tradition that considered the body evil. It influenced Augustine and caused a lot of antagonism toward sexuality and the body in Christian tradition.

The key to Gnosticism is not the archetype of spiritual warfare but the archetype of initiation, as seen in New Age occult groups that show a lot of gnostic emphasis today. The main theme of the New Age movement is initiation, and it tones down any idea of spiritual warfare (see Moore 2001). Although using New Age crystals might seem to relate to the imagery of light and darkness, their devotees really don't want to talk about the shadow side of life or any life-threatening struggle against evil.

Here the New Age point of view differs greatly from the Jungian point of view. New Age people sometimes celebrate Carl Jung in a shallow sort of way, but they are not really Jungians when they refuse to face the shadow side of human society and personality. No Jungian worthy of the name, who tries to stand in the tradition pioneered by Carl Jung, would ever underestimate the power of evil. That was one of his main gifts. We need to collect everything Jung said about evil in one volume, because that has not been done yet, and then we can see better how much importance he put on dealing with it, and how different Jungians are from people who do not take evil seriously (see Stein 1995).

Gnosticism does draw some from the Persian tradition, but from the Jungian point of view you have to ask the prior question, "What archetypal structures in the psyche does Gnosticism draw on?" It certainly draws on the archetype of spiritual warfare, but you would need to know a lot about it to see how it works. Many people who talk about Gnosticism do not know much about this tradition of spiritual warfare, because it is not very popular. They do not want to talk about such things, because that is what fundamentalists talk about.

Audience: From reading *The Gnostic Gospels* by Elaine Pagels, you get things like Jesus being quoted as saying, "If I tell you what is inside me and bring it forth, then that will save me, and if I do not bring forth what is inside me, that is what will kill me." In other words, it puts everything inside, an interesting twist from a psychological point of view, because it seems to address the whole shadow thing, but it may seem foolish to the guy being mugged, or knifed to death, that anything inside could be the source of these kinds of problems.

Moore: Yes, that is the fantasy that you brought all your problems down on yourself. We'll talk later about what we all have inside us that needs to be brought forth consciously.

There are many good treatments of Gnosticism. The book by Elaine Pagels (1979) is wonderful, as well as *The Nag Hammadi Library*, edited by James Robinson (1990). Hans Jonas wrote *The Gnostic Religion* (1958), which gives a lot of the historical background from the intertestamental period. June Singer (1987) has a good chapter on Gnosticism in the book that Murray Stein and I co-edited on *Jung's Challenge to Contemporary Religion* (1987).

This brings us to consider the nature of the task involved in understanding and dealing with the enemy in spiritual warfare. Later we will look at some psychological interpretations of the task and discuss the personal and archetypal aspects of the shadow, before concluding with some observations on how these archetypal realities might be relevant in therapy.

THE WARRIOR FUNCTION

The Japanese tradition says some interesting things about spiritual warfare. For people who are studying the warrior archetype, I like to recommend a popular management book called *Waging Business Warfare* by David Rogers (1988). It explains how the Japanese samurai tradition embodied the Japanese fascination with war and the warrior. The samurai were medieval Japanese knights who developed a form of fencing with swords into a martial art called Kendo that emphasized spiritual warfare. Kendo means "the way of the sword," but it teaches that the greatest enemy of the great swordsmen is an inner enemy, the ego, and that before you cut anything or anyone else, you must cut your own ego. I was fortunate to have a black belt Kendo practitioner as a friend who helped me realize how Japanese martial arts embodied this philosophy.

Many other traditions also contain the idea of dealing with the inner enemy before you deal with the outer enemy. Islam, for example, has the concept of *jihad.* Contrary to what many people think, Islam teaches there are two jihads, two spiritual warfares that are basically the same but linked inwardly. Mohammed is quoted as saying that the lesser jihad is the fight against evil and unrighteousness out there in the world, while the greater jihad is the war against evil within, the part of you that tries to make you unfaithful and not a loyal servant of Allah and truth and justice.

Many traditional teachers had a sophisticated understanding that "facing the dragon" was a primal inner struggle of spiritual life, though with many outer expressions as well. It was never merely inner, never merely a matter of "integrating your shadow." We have much work to do in the outer world as well.

You should all be familiar with the archetype of the hero and how the functioning of the hero archetype is imaged in the context of a cataclysmic struggle. Joseph Campbell's book *The Hero with a Thousand Faces* (1949) is a wonderful treatment of hero mythology (see also Miller 2000). Jungians talk a lot about the hero as the archetypal ground of the developing ego in a personality, how the hero struggles greatly against the forces of unconsciousness. Some people say the hero in masculine psychology struggles mainly against the regressive pull of the mother complex, but that is an unfortunate way to think about it, for it also involves the regressive pull to remain in the great "cloud of unknowing" and thus in denial of the destructive forces both within and without.

Human beings have an enormous desire not to know. It is very painful to know. If we did a popularity contest among all the defense mechanisms, the defense mechanism of denial would win hands down. It is the most popular one. Unconsciousness is difficult to deal with, and it takes a heroic struggle in the psyche to develop a strong ego. Certainly anything like an adequate ego function is not automatic. If you have evaluated your own ego function lately, you know that even after much therapy and struggle it is difficult to get yourself conscious and stay awake. This is the primal deep reality in this whole issue of spiritual warfare. It is a struggle against unconsciousness.

Consider, though, how the archetype of the hero differs from the archetype of the warrior. The hero archetype is fundamentally an image of adolescence and the struggle against unconsciousness, so you would not want the hero in charge of all your legions. He might make a good leader after his heroic struggle, but during the struggle itself, he is still trying to come to maturity. The hero journeys toward maturity and responsibility, but until he gets there, he is like the Tom Cruise character in the movie *Top Gun* (1986). For all of his strong characteristics, he cannot be a good flight commander for your air force until he gets some aging and savvy, confronts his grandiosity, and learns more about cooperation and teamwork.

Good warriors, by contrast, have full command of their resources, their gifts, and their abilities, and they can mobilize them, organize them, channel them, and direct them in the service of transpersonal commitments toward transpersonal goals. Studying the history and mythology of generalship also provides a sense of the true warrior's mature deployment of forces and resources in a significant struggle. The true warrior represents mature ego function.[6]

How does the warrior archetype function in the psyche? People without solid relatedness to the warrior within cannot deploy themselves well in whatever they have to do in life. To get it clear psychologically, they go into enormous amounts of ineffectual self-defeating and passive-aggressive behavior. When you relate adequately to your archetypal warrior within, whether you are male or female, you will be more effective and have less trouble with depression. Other people, however, may have more trouble with your aggression!

Try this clinically with the people you are working with. Try to help them in their warrior function. Help them get organized and focused, making plans, solving problems, making strategic and tactical decisions, and moving on them, and see how depressed they stay. You will immediately notice they get less depressed. But to the extent that people cannot act or coordinate action, they will be depressed, passive-aggressive, and anxious.

You can do a lot by accessing the archetype of the warrior. For example, with help from the warrior within, the human psyche always manages to find the enemy and mobilize against it. This is important, because people often have a hard time locating where their primary struggle really is. If you are a practicing counselor or working with people, you will find that a lot of people have never taken the time to raise the question, "Where is my struggle?" They are not clear about what they want to struggle for, toward, or against.

Some people today even suggest that you do not need to struggle, that you should just relax, get a hot tub and enjoy. That is a different archetype, the archetype of the lover, that wants you to get into a hot tub, take off your clothes, get all warm and fuzzy, and not be too task-oriented. It is hard to be task-oriented while in the archetype of the lover. On the other hand, a lot of people do take the warrior into their love life and try to be task-oriented there, but it doesn't work very well.

One way to understand the warrior is to check out the people you work with and ask, "Do they have a real functioning general operating somewhere in their psyche, in their life?" If not, they are probably backing their way through life in a depressed, passive-aggressive mode, and will continue to do so.

Audience: What do you mean by "a functional general"?

Moore: Someone to take charge when there is a clear need, someone to clarify the terrain, make judgments about resources and where one should open an offensive. You cannot do everything at once. You need a capacity to assess, prioritize, focus, mobilize, evaluate, and concentrate. All these things come right out of the archetype of the warrior and the study of the psychology of leadership. All talk about leadership qualities draws upon the archetype of the warrior and the regal archetypes of king or queen. The warrior does not necessarily have anything to do with war at all, but with struggle in general, and being able to focus on objectives and effectiveness.[7]

Audience: Is this regardless of personality type? Would not an intuitive have a different warrior mode than a thinker?

Moore: They would typically have a different way of expressing it, or not expressing it, but a lot of introverted intuitive types are out of touch with their warrior. They sort of wait around, because they expect to intuit their way through the struggles of their life. You can have excellent intuitive knowledge, but it is no substitute for action. There are many things in life, and particularly in individuation, that you simply cannot get without action. If you do not act and face your individuation tasks, then you tend to just sit and do nothing, and consequently, you do not get the transformation you need.[8]

Audience: Are there not types that just inherently find some certain things easier than others?

Moore: Certainly, but sensation types are more in touch with this, and your ESTJ is probably more natural, but these types have limits. I am suspicious of typology in general, because it is too simple. Human beings are not as simple as typology seems to indicate. Each type still has to face the various archetypal structures and the challenge to achieve a more optimal integration.

Audience: But people do have different kinds of personality.

Moore: Yes, they do, largely determined by the structure of the archetypal integration in their personality. But they also have different abilities to be in touch with their surroundings and make accurate, reality-based judgments. People who are paranoid, or otherwise have bad judgment, will tend to misread their surroundings. Any personality can improve its integration through an optimal accessing of the warrior within.

We have to avoid simplistic use of typology because an optimally integrated personality usually transcends the limitations of one particular type. For example, a close study of the biographies of outstanding generals throughout history shows they tended to be very intuitive, but they also tended to be good thinkers in touch with their surroundings. A fully integrated warrior has a mature personality that you cannot expect to be locked into one narrow typological function. Even an intuitive type is better able to assess the shadow of the enemy. It is a subtle thing. Saint Augustine, for example, whatever else you may think about him, was a great person who was a powerful administrator and a leader, yet he was also a mystic, intuitive, and introverted. Powerful historical leaders simply do not fit well into neat typological categories.

A first-rate general often knows what the enemy is thinking, while second-rate ones do not. The overrated British general Bernard Montgomery knew what he was going to do, but he often could not discern what the enemy was going to do. That was one of the greatest problems with his leadership. Military historians have evaluated him badly on that score. A good general anticipates what the enemy is thinking, and he takes that into consideration as part of his decision-making process.

You can see how adaptive this insight is. What does it mean if you cash it out? It means that people with a developed warrior part of their personality are less narcissistic. They are able to have more empathy with the enemy and offer them appropriate respect. The greatest generals have always admired the generals on the other side. There is a wonderful line in the movie *Patton* (1970), which you ought to watch in this context. George C. Scott is incredible as General Patton. You can see Patton's immaturity and narcissistic pathology, but you can also see some of his greatness. In one scene he has just left a great battle where he faced off with the great German general Erwin Rommel and wiped out Rommel's tanks. He stops for a moment and takes down his binoculars and says, "Rommel, you magnificent ———, I read your book!"

A pure narcissist would never have read that book, because he could not give the enemy that much admiration and credit. A warrior like Patton attained the level where he never underestimated his enemies, never disrespected them, but learned everything he could about them.

Underestimating what you are dealing with is one of the marks of grandiosity and immaturity. This is really important in the human psyche and in psychotherapy. Both therapists and people in therapy make mistakes about this. They underestimate what they are dealing with and have what I call "flights into health." The flight into health is where people say, "I am all better now, no more symptoms," and they quit right at the time when they were getting somewhere. That is the same kind of thing as underestimating the power and cunning of the great enemy within.

This leads us to a discussion of the personal and archetypal aspects of the shadow, before concluding with some observations on the therapeutic relevance of these archetypal realities.

Integrating the Personal Shadow

The Jungian concept of the shadow, and the whole struggle toward consciousness, is a contemporary reappropriation of all the light-and-darkness imagery in religious traditions and mythology. Jung makes good use of this imagery as background for his goal of an increased awareness that brings light into the recesses of the personality so we can see relationships between the various aspects of the personality. He describes the mighty struggle going on in your psyche between your shadow and your ego personality, and how you must get them to stop warring and start communicating as partners and brothers. The struggle is like the twinship images of Cain and Abel, Jacob and Esau, which all reflect the inner alienation and need for reconciliation.

In the Jungian psychology of the shadow, your goal is to bring about mutual respect and peace negotiations in the inner civil war in your soul. This is certainly true for personal developmental issues and splitting off childhood pain and traumas. The whole idea of healing means bringing these denied feelings and experiences back into awareness, and not allowing them to split us right down the middle. The integration of the personal shadow brings peace, harmony, and integration to the psyche. That is how Jungians deal with the mythic struggle between light and darkness. The psychological task in analysis is to help the light win by including many things that were formerly excluded. You can equate light with awareness.

The darkness of unconsciousness is very strong, but the light of awareness pushes it back. In Jung's morality of awareness, the struggle for individuation is a struggle for light, a struggle to get conscious, to get more of your experience and personality out of the dark so it can be respected, loved, accepted, and affirmed. The challenge is relating consciously to the depth and complexity of who you are. Like Jean Bolen says, you can have your inner get-togethers where all your warring family members can come together and have a family council meeting. All the different parts of your shadow get together and talk to each other, and say, "Okay, I want this, and you want that, now what can we agree on here?" This is like trying to get mutual respect and peace talks going around your inner round table. That is all true and very important.

The Archetypal Shadow

The archetypal shadow is another idea we need to reflect on. Is the shadow all personal or not? What does it mean to talk about the archetypal shadow? Can you distinguish between the archetypal shadow and the personal shadow? Many Jungians don't make that distinction, of course, but I am one Jungian who takes archetypes very seriously, as well as the distinction between the personal psyche and the objective psyche, the collective unconscious.

Let me give you a quick sense of what I mean by archetypal shadow. All Jungians who have studied developmental psychology know how an archetypal configuration can come in and take over a personality and possess it. This happens all the time in one-sided personalities where the person has been hurt developmentally and the resulting ego is weak. The more you were hurt in your early development, the weaker your ego structure will be, and the more likely an archetypal pattern will colonize you and derail your individuation. That is a fundamental assumption of my neo-Jungian psychoanalytic theory.

Jung taught that archetypes have their own shape and objective psychic reality. The mother archetype is the mother archetype whether it possesses you or not, and the child archetype is the child archetype whether it manifests overtly in your psyche right this minute or not. There is compelling evidence that some archetypal elements of the shadow are not simply split-off personal experiences, but represent common human experiences that the religious traditions associated with an archetypal adversary, whether it be Satan or Iblis or Ahriman.

The study of human apprehensions of evil is interesting, because people in very different places have much agreement about its principles and dynamics, and how it works. I have studied the history of human images of evil in great depth for a long time, and I teach courses at the doctoral level on the images of evil in culture and psychopathology. This is complicated, but I can summarize it a bit. Evil is very much antilife. It is full of hate. It tries to destroy relatedness. It uses deceit, lying, and illusion. In fact, almost all folklore presents evil as deceit and lying and a master of illusion. Evil hates the light, and even loses its power when light is around. Evil cannot stand to be exposed, and it hates human community for that reason. Evil wants to get you alone and isolate you. It also wants to get you in the dark.

Popular culture is wonderfully insightful about this. Popular horror films, for instance, are wonderful about picking up on these motifs about the marks of evil, and they all agree. Evil wants to get you in the dark, wants to get you alone, wants you to think it is not coming from that direction, because as soon as you think it is not coming from that direction, that is the direction it will come from.

Several recent films give a wonderful treatment of these archetypal mythic dimensions and assessment of evil. *The Thing* (1982) starred Kurt Russell. Another example is *The Invasion of the Body Snatchers* (1978), not the early version but the recent remake with Donald Sutherland. Take a look at these films. It is worthwhile just to see Kurt Russell or Donald Sutherland dramatizing these psychological realities.

These films show evil destructiveness operating consistently like it does in Dracula and werewolf movies and stories of folklore, fairy tales, and religious traditions. We cannot attribute all this consistency back to personal creativity. Some of it must come from a specieswide intuition and be archetypal in nature.

The evil force always comes from the outside but is inside you before you know it. You always think it is out there knocking at the door, but it is already inside. The most terrifying thing about "the thing" or the alien is that you can't tell who has it and who doesn't. You don't even know whether it has already possessed you or not. Though "the thing" refers to unconscious grandiose energies that threaten to destroy us, in the mythic imagination the whole struggle occurs in terms of apocalyptic light-darkness imagery. Whenever it is darker, "the thing" attacks. Whenever the people are isolated, it gets them.

So much consistency in all these traditions raises the probability that these archetypal dimensions of human destructiveness go beyond the fact that someone had a bad mother. Personal developmental failures, and nurturing failures, just like everything else about families, may come from archetypal energies that families unconsciously welcomed into the home in an unregulated way. Personal traumas make people vulnerable at various times in their lives to possession by certain archetypal patterns of destruction that have their own organization and agency and do not derive simply from less than perfect parenting. These objective psychic realities are alien to the personal and family history, and yet are so common that humans throughout the world recognize them when confronted with them.

Freud, as a non-Jungian example, long recognized *thanatos* and *eros* as two opposing drives in human life, based on his clinical observations. He used *thanatos*, the Greek word for death, to describe something he commonly saw in people, not exactly a "death-wish" in the simple popular sense, but more like an instinct toward death. Freud observed this and tried to explain it, but people told him it sounded too mystical, so he dropped it, but his original observation still stands. He saw something in people that pushes them toward destruction, that tries, in our terms, to get them to leave therapy right when they are getting better, but without consolidating their positive changes.

In other words, something always seems to intervene the minute you begin making progress. Consider, for example, a person who never had a decent relationship in his life, and just when he finds the right person in a relationship that could go somewhere, a person who will not abuse him but really love him, that is exactly when he comes up with some reason not to have anything more to do with that person. It is so amazing. I see this in people that I am working with all the time, and if you are a therapist you see it in the people you are working with.

Now if you saw only a few people like this, you might say it comes from their unique experiences with their parents, but if you see it operating this way over and over again in many different kinds of people, then it looks less like personal experience and more like they all read the same manual on "How Not to Survive," or "How Not to Thrive in Life," or "How to Self-Destruct." If you work with a lot of substance abusers, or people with bad self-hate patterns, and you study their families, it is hard to reduce it simply to saying their mothers made some bad mistakes and now we have this mega self-destructing ball of flesh here in the office crying out from the pain and pleading to us for help.

Another view of this comes from the British object-relations theorists in the Fairbairn-Guntrip school (see Hazell 1995 and 1996). They talk about the anti-libidinal ego, for which there is a whole literature. The anti-libidinal ego should be translated "anti-life ego." Part of a person's psyche is hell-bent on destroying her and not allowing her to have any love, not allowing her to have any trust, not allowing her to have any successful transformation of her patterns of relatedness and her patterns of human interaction. The very minute she gets involved in relationships that are more hopeful, this thing mobilizes, gets aggressive, and seeks to destroy the new relationship. It strikes me that there is a need for deeper reflection on what this is that gets constellated.

This has an interesting parallel with studies of the psychology of the myth of the birth of the hero, because every time the divine child gets born, what happens? The armies of Herod or Pharaoh are mobilized, and they seek to attack the baby. That is archetypal and objective, and it suggests that anytime there is new life or progress being made in the personality, you can expect a counter-attack that has nothing to do with the parents' lack of quality. It may well be that Herod's armies, or Pharaoh's armies, or the armies of demons that attacked the Buddha, or the armies of Ravana that attacked Rama in the Ramayana epic, that all those armies refer to the same archetypal reality, psychic realities that are archetypal, not personal, and are out to stop you when you start making progress.

All the different religious traditions have been convinced about this reality. We moderns are the only people who have not accepted it, and we have the bomb and pollution instead. Jung believed that when we stop talking about the demons we become more vulnerable to their destructive force.[9]

So I want to suggest that there is more to this archetype of spiritual warfare than simply integrating your personal shadow, or merely learning how to love those denied parts of your personality. It involves learning how to tell the difference between the personal shadow that comes from your individual experience, and the archetypal forces which have access to your psyche from within, that you can never integrate, and had better not try to integrate. Jung discusses this in volume eight of the *Collected Works* in his distinction between personal complexes and what he calls "spirit complexes."

IMAGES OF TRANSPERSONAL ASSISTANCE

Audience: Where does the Resurrection fit in this? It is beyond warfare. The Resurrection ultimately defeats all the forces of evil that participated in the Crucifixion.

Moore: Yes, that is the image of transpersonal forces that do not let evil have the last word. In that image, from the point of view of the ego, you lose, and from the ego's point of view, we do a lot of losing, we do a lot of dying. If you work with people in any depth, you know they are battle-scarred veterans. They have lost a lot of battles, but they have resources that come to their aid that are not just individual resources, but are transpersonal, trans-egoic forces. That is the whole Jungian idea behind the Self with a capital "S." If you are cooperative, the Self with a capital "S" will see to it that you have helpers in your darkest hour. You will not get off scot-free, but in your darkest hour you will have helpers.

Audience: In the Reformed Christian tradition we call it "Providence."

Moore: Providence is parallel to the Jungian concept of synchronicity, the idea that the great General of the universe will not leave anyone without reinforcements.

Audience: This is the Holy Spirit.

Moore: You have a transpersonal Helper available to you. It does not mean you can avoid what you have to do, but you are not in it alone. That is part of the genius of Jung, and one of the things that makes Jungian psychology such a powerful alternative to all other psychologies, for none of them work from the assumption that the ego has help from within the psyche.

Audience: This is a theme in the Bible actually, because many times the warriors thought, "This is the battle where I am going to be defeated," but then something happens to change the course of the battle. Or they thought, "This is a battle we cannot lose," and then they fell on their faces.

Moore: Right, and one of the most interesting things is the image that the outcome of the struggle is not a merely a matter of numbers, and thus not a matter of who seems to have superior force. When these archetypal things get constellated in a certain way, the weaker forces can triumph, like David against Goliath, and there are many other stories with the same theme.

Audience: Like Jesus himself in his humble birth.

Moore: Yes, all these stories are trying to say something to us. You could say, in Jungian terms, that as long as the personal ego does not turn itself away from the presence and guidance of the archetypal Self, that no matter how wounded or weak or imprisoned you may be, and no matter how difficult and hopeless your image of trouble may seem to you to be, there are enduring realities that come to your side and give you a chance to succeed in your struggle.

Notes

1. This material was transcribed and edited from a taped lecture and discussion led by Robert L. Moore at the C. G. Jung Institute of Chicago, Illinois, on February 10, 1988.

2. The current most accessible presentations are probably Vermes (1995, 1997, 2000).

3. Madeleine L'Engle (pronounced len-GAL) wrote the Time Fantasy series in four volumes. These works present love as the only effective weapon in the struggle against darkness, chaos, and evil. L'Engle's sizable body of work continues to get serious attention. See Chase (1995) and Wytenbroek (1995).

4. On Tolkien (1892–1973), see Carpenter (1977) and Becker (1978). On C. S. Lewis (1898–1963), see Walsh (1979), Wilson (1990), and Schultz and West (1998).

5. See 1 Corinthians, chapters 2 and 3, especially 2:1–10 and 3:1–3. Also Hebrews 5:11–14.

6. For a fuller discussion, consult Moore and Gillette (1992).

7. Covey's book, *The Seven Habits of Highly Effective People* (1989), is excellent on this.

8. See my lectures, "The Courage to be Transformed," available from the C. G. Jung Institute of Chicago.

9. Morton Kelsey's book, *Encounter with God* (1988), discusses these cultural movements toward increasing lack of awareness of these realities, but even he does not realize how much more vulnerable moderns are to such invasions than were premodern people. You cannot fight something you cannot discern.

CHAPTER 3

Regulating Dragon Energies

The Challenge of Conscious Ritualization

MANY PEOPLE TODAY REFUSE TO LOOK AT HOW ISSUES of human spirituality relate to such larger problems as pathological tribalism, not because they consider these issues uninteresting or unimportant, but because there is so much denial today about their radical importance for the human future. Many intellectuals unfortunately seem to think that anyone who addresses issues of human spirituality, even the idea that there might be such a thing as "human spirituality," is sort of dreamy and out of contact with reality.[1]

The first thing to discuss, therefore, is why it is so important to address this topic effectively today. After a brief word on my own interest in the topic, I will sketch in broad outline what I see as the main spiritual and psychological challenges today. I will describe some new resources now available that make it possible for us to think in a more systematic and realistic way about facing these tasks. We now have the resources to begin facing the fundamental spiritual tasks of our species. This is not something, in my view, that has been the case very long.

Let me start with a word about myself and my interest in this topic. I am a Jungian psychoanalyst, but I am also an Adlerian analyst, and my first book was a Freudian book. I have continued to study contemporary Freudian theory with the school of self psychology in the tradition of Heinz Kohut. I consider myself a neo-Jungian now, however, and am happy to make that claim, because I feel that Jung's theoretical paradigm is far and away superior to any psychology that is remotely in second place. That is not to say that it is the archetypal psychology, because I do not believe in an "archetypal psychology," but I do believe that Jungian psychology can and should be an empirical, scientific psychology of the archetypes. I want to make it clear that I am not a Hillmanian; I am a neo-Jungian. There is a big difference between a neo-Jungian psychoanalyst and a post-Jungian "archetypal psychologist." Theoretical assumptions really matter when it comes to the effectiveness of our integrative interpretations of interdisciplinary research.

I am also a professor of psychology and religion at Chicago Theological Seminary where I teach psychology, religion, and spirituality to rabbis, priests, and other clergy and interested laity. I have worked in this area for a long time. In the summer of 1965, when I was still in my twenties, a professor set me off on this journey by introducing me to Alfred North Whitehead, Carl Jung, and Ludwig Von Bertalanffy, the founder and primary theoretician of General Systems Theory. The experience really blew my mind, and I have never been the same since. I have spent a ridiculous amount of money, time, energy, blood, sweat, and tears, trying to figure out the implications of these theorists for psychology and the spiritual life. I don't regret it, but it is amazing to think back on all that has happened to me as I've continued working in these areas.

I also edit the Paulist Press series on Jung and spirituality, which provides a forum for bringing the world's spiritual traditions into dialogue by using Jungian psychoanalysis as a holding environment, a way of providing a container for in-depth discussion for people who will not dialogue any other way (Moore 1988, Moore and Meckel 1990, Meckel and Moore 1992).

Another proposed project of the Institute for World Spirituality is the *International Directory of World Religions*. Even today, you still could not contact all the religious leaders in the world if you wanted to, because no one reference work tells you how to reach them, who they are, and where they are. If this project succeeds, we will for the first time in history have a reference work for contacting every religious group on earth.[2]

These projects symbolize something important happening in the world today. If Teilhard de Chardin was correct that there is a burgeoning planetary consciousness, then you would assume one spin-off from that would be some improvement in communications. We may soon have much greater potential for communication among the various religious of the world.[3]

Why is it so important to address these spiritual and psychological issues that others choose to deny? Because they are so basic to human existence that if we do not deal with them adequately, we may lose the opportunity to deal with any of the other issues. The survival of our species and all our relations may hang in the balance.

We must try to understand the psychodynamics of why people avoid discussing the relation of spirituality to such problems as pathological tribalism. There are clear psychological reasons for this avoidance that have to do with the infantile grandiosity in our psyches. It overstimulates our grandiose energies when we start looking at the large problems facing humanity. We become very anxious. It's like having a 300-pound St. Bernard jumping around in your head. Your defenses just shut it down. This is a common understanding in psychoanalytic self psychology. What happens when you start letting yourself feel grandiose enough to address some truly large human problems? This is not anything fancy, just basic self psychology, but we need to understand how it works to keep us from addressing significant human problems.

My conviction is that we must intervene in these dynamics so we can ask and address these important questions. They require that we develop the awareness to face them and formulate some effective strategies for dealing with them.

There is currently little interest in this most important topic because the denial is so massive on these fronts. We have such fear of being overwhelmed by our grandiosity, our messianic complexes, that we shy away from this. We would rather watch soap operas or something. It is much more self-soothing.

It seems to me that the contemporary world faces a decisive human crisis. Contrary to what arrogant secularism would have us believe, secularism has *not* brought great progress in a long-term prognosis for humanity. All you have to do is get serious about the ecological problems of this planet, and look closely, not at some speculation, but at the hard data we already have, about what our species is doing to other species, and what the voracious, insatiable appetites of human narcissism are doing to this planet. We have enough information now, if the denial level were not so high, to make it clear to anyone with any interest in it that this cannot be just another academic topic, something to do if you are bored and want to do something new to cope with your boredom. This is a survival business, a radically serious survival business.

The general failure to understand this problem is a mark of the pall of enchantment that hangs over our planet. The metaphors you need to understand what is happening in the human consciousness today are available more in the work of J. R. R. Tolkien than in many other places. Our planet lives under an enormous cloud of enchantment of consciousness, a massive denial that Ernest Becker describes in his work, *The Denial of Death* (1975). It is a lot more serious, however, than Becker points out, because it is not just a denial of death, but a denial of all sorts of serious and worsening problems. Our denial of the ecological situation is a central issue, yet many well meaning social critics refuse to look at the psychological nature of such problems. Some of my friends in concerned and committed activist organizations think that psychological analysis is actually the enemy of finding solutions. They think anyone with deep interest in psychology must be a total "navel gazer," trying more to get away from the world's problems than to solve them.

Some of these people believe that the world's problems would disappear if they could just translate all religious categories into Marxist terms and get everyone to be socialists. They assume, for example, that Marxists would never engage in cocaine trafficking, that a Marxist country would never have to shoot its generals for smuggling in cocaine, and that Marxists would never execute people who were longing for freedom. Did you know that? We would not have to execute students, or shoot them in the streets, if we were Marxists. You can go on and on with that, and it makes me sick, because it shows such an incredible naiveté about the realities of life. They need to read Reinhold Niebuhr's classic works on the dynamics of human pride that afflict all ideologies left and right (Niebuhr 1941–1943). The human predicament does not result from having the wrong ideology.

Our task today is to turn away from what Robert Bly (1973, 1990) would call a "naive male" or "naive female" approach to the human situation. Bly irritates a lot of people by pointing out some of the horrible things going on out there in the world. In a significant way, poetry and folklore and myth have always pointed these things out to us, and it didn't matter what the ideology was. People always find a way to corrupt it for narcissistic, antisocial purposes. The pervasiveness of these problems makes psychoanalytic interpretation and Jungian reflection especially important for understanding the issues and finding potential solutions.

Some people think we need to go back to premodern tribal cultures and forms to find solutions for our problems, but they differ on one thing: which tribe to go back to. We have people who want to go back to the Hopi, to the Mayans, to the Dagara, to the Navaho, and so on. I get letters from people in all these tribes who want to write books about their tribes for the Jung and Spirituality series. The number of different spiritual tribes out there is enormous.

First, you have to get a feeling for what tribal culture is like. For the tribe in the premodern world, the tribe itself *was* the human species. Anyone outside the tribe was not human. The movie *Little Big Man* (1970) showed this by translating the Indian language name for tribal members as "human beings," thus implying that people outside the tribe were not "human beings." This is an enormously important point, because such a perspective is acceptable only as long as your tribe has no contact with other tribes. When another tribe shows up, the genocidal impulse emerges.

Just the other night I saw the movie *The Lost Horizon* (1937) for the first time. Deep in the mountains of the Himalayas a little Tibetan paradise exists called Shangri-La, and you cannot get there from here. You can be kidnapped and your pilot can die, and you can crash and find yourself there, but it is surrounded by mountains and storms and snow, and you ordinarily cannot get in there from the outside world. Tribalism in Shangri-La is fine, because the people do not have to deal with anyone from the outside.

This was the situation of many tribes for a long time. We still find tribes in the jungle that have no contact with other tribes. So they have no theological problems about it, or questions like, "What about those other people?" Like "Where did Adam and Eve's children find people to marry?"

Increased contact between people of different tribes, however, made conflict an increasingly important and problematic issue. Note, for example, how conflicting tribal mythologies fuel violence and terrorism in the Middle East.

The history of human warfare, however, shows that such conflicts did not always lead tribes into unlimited war and destruction. Some people may consider it bad news, or even impossible news, that all humans have the warrior archetype inside them, but it resides in the physiological hardware, not in the cultural software. Whatever the warrior sees, it either wants to fight or protect. That is what warriors do. That has always been true for humans. But premodern tribal cultures had rituals designed to limit aggression. The rituals of warfare had one purpose: to limit, contain, and control war.

Modern warfare is far from being an improvement. The increasing technological modernization of warfare activities constantly lowers the level of consciousness about ritualization in war. You cannot go up to the War College today and find a course, "Ritualization of Warfare 301." Nowhere in the curriculum does it say, "These are the rituals we engage in to make sure we don't kill too many of the enemy." That is why nuclear proliferation has occurred to such a degree. We are not satisfied to kill all of our enemies once. We want to be able to kill them as many times as possible. This kind of madness is the result of an invasion by unconscious archetypal energies.

The history of warfare and ritualization in warfare shows what an aberrant approach we have to this today. Our species is in a near psychotic state about it. In the tribal era, we could go to war with rituals that got ourselves all fired up. We knew how to make warriors. We would paint them up, get them to hollering, beating all those drums, making all those war noises, generating all that warrior energy! These indigenous tribes were not just doing the Texas two-step. They didn't get together to dance for fun. It was a solemn ritual process designed to create the consciousness needed for the serious purpose of waging limited war.

When they engaged the enemy, they usually were not interested in destroying the entire tribe. They usually wanted to raid and take some captives for ritual purposes. Some Native Americans called this "counting coup." If you were a superior warrior, you might want to ride your horse over to the other side and touch the horse of the best warrior over there, and then ride back to your own side without anyone being injured. You didn't necessarily always kill your enemy.

I want to emphasize here that the ritual software in tribal cultures put great limitations on the destructiveness of warlike impulses. They also had self-limiting ritual structures to regulate consumption. Some of you may know more about this than I do. Can you give me an example of how tribal cultures regulated consumption? Do you know any examples of that? How did they regulate materialism?

Audience: Nature was a great regulator.

Moore: Yes, nature in one sense is certainly the regulator of last resort, but I'm talking about cultural regulators or ritual regulators. Did you ever hear of *potlatch*? What is it? Can someone define it?

Audience: Isn't that a great giveaway, where people come from all over and you give away what you have to them, to show how wealthy you are, how powerful, how generous, and so on.

Moore: Yes, it's a significant ritual occasion. You build up some wealth, you get so many horses or pigs, or whatever, but there comes a time when you do not want to keep on accumulating, so you throw a party to give the surplus away. We still have some of that in our party giving today. To throw a good party, you need some of the primitive energy of gift giving in your psyche. We don't know enough about the ancient psychology of gift giving, but it relates to this archetypal theme. If looked at superficially, it may appear as an arrogant act, but not if you understand its ritual and archetypal foundation. It is what has to be done to create a world, create a cosmos. It manifests the generosity of the archetypal king and queen. All of this relates to the archetype of king and queen.

In summary, premodern cultures often used conscious ritualization to put limits on the kind of aggressive and acquisitive behavior that flourishes today without any such limits. Some rituals in tribal culture limited aggression, and other rituals limited conspicuous consumption and its results. Modern culture today, in sharp contrast, has no effective rituals that limit aggression, and no effective rituals that limit conspicuous consumption and acquisition.

Humans always engage in ritualization, either consciously or unconsciously. What I mean by ritual is someone taking conscious responsibility for leading a group to do things that need to be done. Conscious ritual leadership is something far different from acting out or pseudo-ritualization. Many of these archetypal acting-out ritual forms are not conscious or contained. That is to say, leaders may follow certain ritualized behaviors without understanding the ritual purposes of what they are doing.

For example, our leaders in the Vietnam War did limit aggression in a certain way, but they didn't know what they were doing in any kind of conscious psychological ritual sense. The decisions not to bomb certain areas were not made on the basis of ritual judgments, though they might have been grounded in some unconscious awareness.

Jungian psychology stresses the need to relate consciously to the archetypal patterns and energies. Jungian thought requires an ethic of awareness. It is not enough to act out obsessive, compulsive rituals. The archetypal configurations that we do not ritualize consciously, we are condemned to act out unconsciously. That is a fundamental premise of all my work now, and it has enormous social, political, and ethical implications for global culture.

In an unpublished manuscript entitled "The Last Rite," Douglas Gillette and I argue that there is an unconscious archetypal pressure toward total war that the world will act out unless a new planetary spiritual consciousness develops and intervenes to deal with the pressure. Some kind of great cleansing and spiritual transformation of Planet Earth seems guaranteed by the mounting pressure of grandiose energies in the human psyche. We see two alternatives: (a) the human species will act out its grandiose energies and get "purified" in a great fireball, a third World War, or (b) we will learn consciously how to sacrifice our infantile grandiosity and take conscious responsibility for making the changes we need to realize a great spiritual transformation. Here the deconstructionists are our allies by putting limits on literalism, for we must not take literally the need to immolate and dismember the human species.[4] The fundamentalist eagerness for Armageddon is simply an unconscious literalization of the imperative for transformation.

The apocalypse myth rests on the insistent archetypes of death and rebirth that you find in the dreams of children all over the world. The myth of a great conflagration occurs in every major tradition of world mythology. An appendix to our manuscript gives fifty pages of quotations from these myths of a great fire.

Those who work and think in a Jungian framework cannot ignore these archetypal imperatives in the psyche. Myths for a Jungian theorist are not the same as myths for some academic mythologists. Jungians know that these myths are psychoactive whether anyone else realizes it or not, whether anyone else likes it or not. You cannot avoid the influence of archetypes, because they are in your hardware. You only have the two alternatives of relating to them consciously and responsibly, or acting them out unconsciously. That's my basic assumption. If we choose the latter, the fundamentalists will lead us into the abyss.

Even those parts of the tribal rituals that provoke disgust in us today had an important role in limiting aggression and destruction. We moderns may frown morally when we learn they sacrificed their captives and ate them, for example, but it was usually only a few people, and then they would not conduct any more raids for a while. They usually did not get into a stance of having to kill off all the members of the opposing tribe. Hatred was somewhat contained. In any case, the primitive sacrifices still seem morally superior to the brutal and grotesque genocidal practices of modern warfare. The modern ego apparently finds it hard to face the fact that in our wars we engage unconsciously in large-scale human sacrifice (see Williams 1991, Bailie 1995).

Audience: When you talk about the importance of consciously ritualizing, does that mean ritualizing with understanding?

Moore: Yes, the ritual has to be conscious and led by a ritual elder. First we need an understanding of how the plumbing of human consciousness works, and how it feeds into social, intergroup, interreligious, and international relationships. Then we must have conscious ritual leadership.

Audience: But how was it possible to ritualize with understanding in the premodern world? You are not promoting a return to that premodern kind of ritualization, are you? I am trying to understand the difference.

Moore: Okay, let me address that some more. This is one of the things scholars of premodern tribal cultures have discovered that was not understood by early Christian anthropologists who assumed Christianity was superior to the tribal cultures in every way. Of course, this seems like embarrassing arrogance to us today, because they really didn't understand them at all. They didn't realize the incredible sophistication of tribal ritual elders and their ritual processes, and their relationship to consciousness.

Most tribal cultures were, in fact, light years ahead of us in their understanding of the relationship between ritualization and consciousness. Few psychologists and psychoanalysts today know anything about it. Only a handful of people in the world are even studying how ritual relates to psychological processes, as in Victor Turner's work. Some sophisticated psychologists are only now beginning to realize that transference might actually be a ritual phenomenon, and the psychoanalyst a ritual elder in a transformative process. The classic Freudian point of view was that anyone engaged in ritual was just crazy. It is just embarrassing how naive we are on this.

Nonetheless, the cutting edge in psychoanalytic theory today is to understand that ritualization processes affect the human psyche. The great breakthrough came when Erik Erikson began to point out ritualization in the psyche. We have made a lot of progress since then, but not a lot in terms of what needs to be done. Much of my own work has been in this area.

Take hypnosis, for example, an old ritual phenomenon. Modern Christian antagonism toward magic is based on some early anthropologists who did not understand magic at all. Magic is nothing more than understanding the relationship between what you do in ritual and the kind of consciousness that issues from it. If you were an old tribal medicine man and you realized it was time for a war party, you knew the ritual for creating a warrior. When all the young warriors came back home, you knew the ritual for turning those warriors back into herdsmen again. You had to teach them how to take care of all those horses they stole during the war!

By contrast, think about what happened to our Vietnam War veterans. Our hospitals all over the country are full of young warriors, not so young now, because we failed them. They were made into warriors by incompetent ritual elders who were ritually tone-deaf, a bunch of drill sergeants who knew how to turn people into "shadow warriors" who did not know the moral responsibilities of a true warrior. When the young warriors came home, we failed to bring them together for a dance where they could dance their way out of being warriors and back into being herdsmen. We scattered them instead into VA hospitals all across the country. We knew how to make them killers, but we did not know how to dance them into being civilians who could deal effectively with their issues, and have families, and build communities.

These young men know that something is wrong. If you ever work with any of them or get to know them, you will find that they know they were betrayed by their leaders. The great tragedy is that we have not done enough work on spirituality and ritual to understand how we betrayed them. Among the many other ways, we betrayed them with our ignorance of ritual process.

Audience: Did this also happen after World War II, and if not, what was the difference then?

Moore: This happens after every modern war, but with some differences. After World War II we still had some vestiges of a religious order more or less in place, and the young soldiers could come back feeling they had fought in a moral war, whether that was true or not. They could still come back into a partially intact cosmos, in other words, a world. After World War II, America to some degree still had a sacred canopy. After Korea, it was collapsing, and by the time Vietnam arrived, we no longer had a functional sacred canopy. In the process of modernization, the sacred canopy of myth has collapsed, and that means we have nothing to return home to.[5]

Today we no longer have even a tribal cosmos. This is like the American Indian whose tribal cosmos collapses on him, with nothing left but a self-destructive use of alcohol, drugs, and gambling. This collapse, however, is happening to all of us today, not just to the American Indians. We are all addicted to self-medication now, what I call the "demonic sacraments."

Audience: One way to regulate our consumption through ritual might be for President Bush to offer Poland some of our Fortune 500 executives for a few years to revitalize the Polish economy.

Moore: There are many possible ways to imagine ritual. It is helpful and instructive to engage in creative reflection on this important common task. Intelligent people everywhere should consider what new concrete actions and ritualizations would help achieve global spiritual transformation.

Suppose, for instance, that you belonged to a brainstorming group looking for possible solutions, and I said to you, "Okay, team, our task now is to formulate a new strategy for developing human consciousness and behavior in these problem areas. What concrete rituals would you recommend for creating a new global awareness to limit aggression and consumption?" This is, I think, an important task of the highest priority for the human future. If people really want to do something concrete to solve these serious problems, they must look not merely to economic and political theory, but to what they can contribute personally toward spiritual transformative leadership.

Audience: What function do professional sports such as football play? Would that be a ritualization?

Moore: Yes, sports are an unconscious ritualization to inhibit aggression. Our most aggressive violent sports are unconscious ritualizations. They are really acting out, but they are better than nothing, because if you were to shut down professional sports in this country for a year, the enormous increase in violence and violent crime would blow your mind, maybe literally.

When the leaders of culture forget how to dance, or forget how to throw a dance, what do we turn to? The best we have today is the Grateful Dead and Willie Nelson. They still know how to throw a dance, and it works for a while, but it doesn't work the way we need for it to work. We need conscious, competent, effective ritual leadership addressing our global human situation. Anything less is "rearranging the deck chairs on the Titanic."

Audience: What do you think about Paul Ricoeur?

Moore: Ricoeur's approach is important in terms of deliteralization, but I don't think he provides much of a solution to the larger pressing problems, because his work is not much of a resource for issues of ritual containment. I am a practical man. I am a professor, yes, but I am also an analyst and consultant. I deal with real people and real problems. I don't think a merely academic mode of analysis will solve the problems of the planet. Psychoanalysis limited to the consulting room won't solve the problems either. There simply is not enough time for us to train enough analysts, nor enough money to get people into analysis, to address the human crisis we are in now.

While I am saying what will not work, deconstructionism is not going to work either. There is a lot of fascination today with deconstructionism and postmodernism, the latest fads in criticism and analysis. I agree that we need to get past literalism, but most of the deconstructionists never deal with the issue of how to say something significant and transformative and put things back together. We need to *construct* a cosmos, a habitat for humanity and its relatives.

NOTES

1. The material in chapters 3 through 8 and chapter 10 comes from edited transcripts of six sessions of lecture and discussion led by Robert Moore on Saturday and Sunday, July 15–16, 1989, at the C. G. Jung Institute in Chicago, Illinois. The program was entitled "Jungian Psychology and Human Spirituality: Liberation from Tribalism in Religious Life." This chapter represents the opening session on Saturday morning, July 15, 1989.

2. This research was carried out by Dr. J. Gordon Melton, author of the much acclaimed *Encyclopedia of American Religions*. Unfortunately, lack of adequate funding delayed completion of this visionary project. Potential donors to its completion should contact Dr. Melton directly.

3. The Council for the World Parliament of Religions has done important work on this task.

4. For a recent treatment of this theme, see Edward Edinger, *Archetype of the Apocalypse: A Jungian Study of the Book of Revelation* (1999) and Moore and Douglas Gillette, "The Last Rite" (unpublished manuscript, 1989).

5. Chapter 4 looks at Eliade's idea of the cosmos as a world where the sacred canopy has not collapsed. See also Peter L. Berger, *The Sacred Canopy: Elements of a Sociological Theory of Religion* (1967) and Peter L. Berger, Brigitte Berger, and Hansfried Kellner, *The Homeless Mind* (1973).

Modern Secularism Fuels Pathological Narcissism

Apart from God everything is alien and remote and is held together simply by force. Satan by dint of his superior spiritual powers has succeeded in leading men astray by suggesting to them that they will become as gods. But by the pursuit of evil and by the substitution of himself for God, man, so far from becoming the God-like being of his dreams, becomes the slave of his lower nature, and, at the same time, by losing his higher nature becomes subject to natural necessity and ceases to be spiritually determined from within.

—Nicolas Berdyaev, *Freedom and the Spirit*

THE HEALERS, THE RITUAL ELDERS – WHAT I WOULD CALL the magi – have always been aware that you need to have a diagnosis before you can start a treatment. Some people in psychotherapy differ with that today, but I choose to go against their opinions and stay with the wisdom of the vast majority of the human community. We need to understand the plumbing of this problem. The exciting thing to me is that a number of scholarly analyses have appeared in recent years which, when put together, present a very coherent picture of our situation. This chapter introduces some of the scholars who show us how to diagnose modernity, and then it describes how their interpretations relate to the new contemporary crisis in unconscious grandiosity.[1]

Diagnosing the Modern Secular Loss of the Sacred

First is Peter Berger, one of the great contemporary sociologists for anyone interested in this material. Berger studied how modernization led to fragmentation in human personality and culture in such books as *The Homeless Mind* (Berger, Berger, and Kellner 1973), *A Rumor of Angels* (1969), *The Sacred Canopy* (1967), and *The Heretical Imperative* (1979). His work provides a sophisticated sociology-of-knowledge critique of modernity that parallels Eliade and a number of others. We have available today some very sophisticated studies of how the modernization process has influenced our psychological functioning.

Another scholar that many Jungians do not like, but I increasingly admire, is Peter Homans. Some dislike him because he used a Kohutian self psychology approach to understand the conflict between Freud and Jung, and he pointed to Jung's narcissistic pathology which, in my view, was substantial. It is important to understand that most people have narcissistic pathology, so this is not to dismiss Jung. We all have narcissistic problems. Someone has suggested that we need a "Humans Anonymous Twelve Step Program," to help everyday people deal with their residual narcissistic pathology, and I agree. It's another way of saying that we need a more practical approach to our spirituality if we are to be effective in containing and channeling our grandiose energies.

You should read the book by Peter Homans, *Jung in Context* (1979), for an analysis of what happens in the modernization process. Then read his new book about "modernity and the mourning process" where he elaborates further how he understands the psychology of modernization (Homans 1989). These two books together will give you a more sophisticated understanding of the loss that we suffered as modernization and secularization occurred. What we lost is enormous, contrary to what many modern secularists think.

What was the enormous loss? It was the loss of conscious ritual contact with the realm of the sacred. Before anyone had studied the psychology of this, you could take the line of thought that said, "Now we are free," the French Enlightenment fantasy. "Now we are free of kings, free of priests, and free of all of those religious people telling us what to do. Now we can save humanity and have true civilization." The Enlightenment fantasy was a beautiful, wonderful fantasy. The history of the modern world since that time shows the fantasy of expecting progress without spirituality. "Just get rid of all this God stuff and all this priest nonsense, and we can have progress unlimited." Then, of course, we get the *Titanic,* the unsinkable ship of enlightened secularization and technology.

The pride of the modern West came to its height right before World War I just as our enlightened civilization began to peak out. We believed we had an unsinkable ship with an increasing sophistication among civilizations. Not only were we Christian; we were scientifically advanced. We had the Germany of Goethe and the England of David Hume and the great positivistic nonbelievers, the world that came to be the world of Bertrand Russell. What do we have here?

Audience: "The Proud Tower."

Moore: Yes, so you get the sinking of the unsinkable *Titanic,* and all of a sudden you find yourself in the middle of World War I. Of course, the American Civil War was the beginning of modern warfare, but it was just barely the beginning, because they didn't have real machine guns yet. World War I was the first war to put the full-blown results of modernization into warfare.

Soon after the war ended, grave doubts began to arise about modernized warfare. The great antiwar novel *All Quiet on the*

Western Front was first published in 1929 to express the terror and futility of war. During that time you began to get people like C. S. Lewis and Tolkein, and that whole group of people who began to raise serious questions about modern civilization. "What is wrong here? There is something radically wrong that they didn't tell us about!" You need to look for what is wrong, but you need comparative psychoanalytic theory to get a complete picture.

Mircea Eliade made a major contribution to understanding these issues. Most people have overlooked his most important point – that space and time are heterogeneous for *homo religiosus*, that is, for premodern human beings. There is not just one kind of space and time, not just one world, but two worlds, two kinds of space and time: (a) the world of the profane and (b) the world of the sacred, the world of myth. Eliade's book *The Sacred and the Profane* (1959) lays all this out in a beautiful way that I cannot do adequately here (see Moore 1984, 2001).

This world of *homo religiosus* was not just Christian, however, but existed for eons prior to modernity, including most of human history. In fact, this radical distinction between *ordinary* space and time and *sacred* space and time prevailed throughout human history prior to modernization. Premodern people regularly felt the need to make contact with the divine realm. The liturgical year is a vestige of insights from that time. The Mass also served as a refuge from an ordinary world in which it was important to return often to the sacred center, the *axis mundi*. This world down here is imperfect and human, but the other world is full of numinosity and sacredness and power and grace.

In my view, our survival requires that we get back to the *axis mundi*, the center of the world. We must do this differently, of course, from how premodern people did it, but we *must* get back to the center in order to survive.

What is the sacred center in Christian thought? You Roman

Catholic theologians, what is the center in orthodox Christian theology?

Audience: The sacred coming into the profane?

Moore: Yes. Where does it come in?

Audience: Jesus?

Moore: Yes, and where? This is the literal place for Christians. This is the cross. The blood of Christ, the cup of salvation, the bread of life comes in through the cross of Christ. We are healed, we are fed, and we are made whole through the grace that comes in through the sacred body and blood of Christ. We cannot be made whole without it. That is the primordial intuition in orthodox Catholic Christianity. You may argue about it theologically, and systematic theologians have a field day with it, but psychologically, it is true. The psyche must make connection with a non-ego world through which it can be centered and nourished and made whole in the face of all the brokenness invariably suffered in profane historical clock time. This is the *chronos* time where we are all alienated, as Peter Berger would say, and we are all broken. Or, as Paul Tillich the great theologian put it, where we are all *estranged.* This profane time of estrangement is very different from the kind of time that Christians touch in the Mass and other sacraments.

Muslims have similar experiences with sacred time. I had a great conversation with a Shiite Muslim who was driving my taxi from the airport yesterday, and I learned about Shiite Islam. When the Muslim goes to Mecca and circumambulates the Ka'ba and walks this whole pilgrimage, he is going on a journey to the center. According to Eliade, humans must go on a journey to the center in order to experience renewal and regeneration. That is, until modernity. What happens with modernity? Do you go on journeys to the center?

Audience: Journeys to the outside?

Moore: You journey to the outside, right, in an unconscious

attempt to locate a center, but what about the center in modernity? There isn't one, according to Eliade, and he is absolutely right
about this. When you become truly modern psychologically and
culturally, you cannot find the center anymore. Modern and postmodern cultural blinders render the traditional centers invisible.
Whether or not you agree theologically with orthodox Christian
dogma or ritual is another issue, but Jung thought it accurately
represented psychological reality in many ways.

The two Greek words *chronos* and *kairos* distinguish between
regular, everyday time and special or sacred time. A lot of people
have the wrong idea that *kairos* only refers to special moments,
because it means "fullness of time." There are indeed times when
you experience this fullness in pregnant moments, ready-to-be-
birthed time, but Eliade helps us understand that *kairos* time is
always pregnant and full. It is a misunderstanding to think that
kairos only means a pregnant moment so special that it only comes
once in a thousand or two thousand years. The psychological and
spiritual source of *kairos* is always full. According to Eliade, this is
the sacred. For Jung, it is the *pleroma* (fullness).

Suppose, for example, that I am a primitive herdsman, and I
have a family. Perhaps I'm Abraham wandering around in the
desert, and I'm getting tired of it, tired of feeling lost all the time.
Luckily I happen to know about rituals and divination, so I get
my special goat that was revealed to me in my dreams, and I set
this goat loose, because I know it is a sacred goat who can find the
center of the world. It is an instrument of divination. I don't
know where the sacred spot is, but I believe my goat can find it.
So I let my goat wander around, and we all follow that goat.
When it stops, in the biblical tradition, at a place called Bethel,
we all know that this must be sacred space, the center of the
world, the *axis mundi*. This is where Jacob's ladder is, where traffic takes place between the sacred and profane realms. We offer up

a sacrifice and put up a pile of stones to mark the place or put an altar there.

This is true throughout human experience, no matter what the tradition. They all did this at some level, and still do. You travel around the world as I love to do, and you study every culture on the globe, and I will guarantee that you will find many interesting places where people have done this. Some of them have been there for thousands of years, and they have survived through the different religions that controlled them. Those of us who love Jerusalem will always consider it sacred space whether it is ruled by the Muslims, the Jews, or the Christians. It will always be sacred space, a representation of the *axis mundi,* the spiritual center of the world.

Mecca is the same thing. This great mountain of Islamic pilgrimage was a sacred destination for pilgrims long before the time of Mohammed. From a history of religions point of view, when Mohammed organized what later became known as Islam, he used many things that already existed in ritual practice at sacred centers. Eliade describes how the symbolism of the sacred stone at the heart of Islam preexisted. Harry Partin (1967) wrote a great dissertation on the Islamic pilgrimage that was never published, and I think it should be. He traced the sacred stone worship that preceded the pilgrimage to Mecca to the forms that exist today. Do you follow what I am getting at? There is always this human journey to the sacred center.

Another good reference on this is Victor Turner's essay, "The Center Out There: Pilgrim's Goal," in *History of Religions* (1973). Before Victor Turner's death, he and his wife Edith also published *Image and Pilgrimage in Christian Culture* (1978), but its understanding of pilgrimage applies to every human culture, because they all have pilgrimages. If you have a Jungian point of view to complete the psychological side, then you have an integrated and holistic understanding of this.

So what is lost when modernization occurs? We are always wanting to be autonomous, right? We want to cut the umbilical cord and tie it off right here and now. Autonomy is our goal. No more conflicts between autonomy, shame, and doubt, for those of you who know Erikson. We get rid of all those Catholics, all those priests, and especially all those nuns we went to parochial school with. "I had shame and doubt when I had them, but now I have autonomy. Where they wanted me to have poverty, chastity and obedience, now I am going to have prosperity, sex, and autonomy. Get rid of spirituality and you get the goodies." That is the modern fantasy, but we did not anticipate the rise of the culture of narcissism with its worsening epidemic of pathological grandiosity.

Understanding Grandiosity and Its Impact

Contemporary psychoanalytic research has led us full circle on these matters. We are now beginning to understand that contemporary culture has this one little fly in the ointment: the epidemic of unregulated human grandiosity.

Every concerned person needs to stop and think about this question. Why might grandiosity become a growing problem in modern, secular culture? What is there about secular-oriented culture that might cause an increase in problems of psychological grandiosity? Not theological problems. Forget theology for a moment. This is just a question about the psychology of narcissism. We can bracket theological issues here and talk about psychodynamics.

Chicago is the center of a school of psychoanalytic thought grounded in the work of Heinz Kohut whose psychology of narcissistic personality disorders created great conflict in Freudian circles. Kohut noticed that grandiosity, rather than improving your sex life, either makes you impotent or makes you so promiscuous that you cannot sustain relationships and you put yourself in danger of getting AIDS and dying. In other words, grandiosity tends to destroy you if you don't face up it and learn how to regulate it.

Another example is the work that many therapists do with addictive disorders of various kinds. Jerome Levin's book *Treatment of Alcoholism and Other Addictions* (1987) shows how infantile grandiosity generates addictions and compulsions. This is Kohutian, not Jungian, but it just happens to agree with Jung. Levin thinks that all addictions and compulsive behaviors reveal an incorrect relationship to one's grandiose self organization. That is interesting to me, and I believe he is right (see also Levin 1993).

Audience: What exactly do you mean? Can you give me a quick definition of exactly what you mean by "infantile grandiosity."

Moore: Your ego becomes so inflated that you act as if you thought you were God. A more detailed definition is given under "narcissistic personality disorder" in *The Diagnostic and Statistical Manual of Mental Disorders* of the American Psychiatric Association. My research finds intrusions of grandiose energies in all four major forms of archetypal energy (see chapter 6).

Very simply, "grandiosity" means you have larger fantasies and wishes for yourself than your real life experience can support, so they either make you *manic,* running around trying to keep up with their demands, or they make you *depressed* because your desires are so high and unachievable that it soon seems useless to try to do anything at all.

A manic state exists when you cannot sleep because your mind is thinking of all the great books you are going to write, or you cannot develop a relationship with one woman because you want to have sex with every woman you know. Or you cannot drink sensibly, because you want to drink everything you can get your hands on. One person said, "If I do not watch my grandiosity, the grandiose lover inside of me wants to drink all of the bourbon they can bottle in Kentucky." People like this are not satisfied with a shot here and there, now and then. They want all of it. Another example of addictive personality manifesting in greed would be someone who takes inordinate risks in gambling on the stock market.

Whether the addiction is sex, money, alcohol, food, or whatever, there is this greedy little god in the psyche, and everyone has it, whether from the point of view of centrist Jungian thought or psychoanalytic self psychology. There is no one alive who does not have a grandiose, exhibitionistic self-organization, an actual psychological structure or entity that thinks it is God. This fascinating thought has many disturbing implications.

The bad news about this grandiosity is that trying to avoid it by being humble only indicates the enormity of your struggle. I hate to disturb anyone's good day, but a really humble person may be having more trouble with grandiosity than someone who thinks they are pretty hot stuff. If you get depressed a lot because you think you are worthless, it indicates a mighty struggle with this little god within. You need to feel like you weigh a thousand pounds in your leaden depression so you won't float off into the sun and be destroyed by an Icarus complex.

From this point of view, what is depression? It is your friend. Thank God for your depression, because it is the ballast on your psychic balloon. Without it, you would be flying into the sun of psychosis. The genius of this recent psychoanalytic work is simple and profound, because it shows that everyone without exception has the same problem of this powerfully burning solar furnace within, what Jung called the archetypal Self.

Different psychoanalytic theories talk about it in many different ways. Adlerian therapists label it the "superiority complex" behind every "inferiority complex," and then try to help you find the ways you think you are better than everyone else. They try to get you to come down off your little throne and join the rest of humanity (Adler 1989). Most theorists agree with the Adlerians that it is simplistic to blame someone morally for being up there on their little high chair.[2]

Traditional religions, by contrast, do tend to blame you moralistically for being up there on your high chair. This creates the irony of one person sitting on a little high chair over there criticizing you for being on your little high chair over here. What traditional spiritualities do not seem to understand is that sitting on a little monk high chair is no more humble than sitting on a little libertine high chair. Spiritual athletes are often just as inflated in their grandiosity as are people who seem just the opposite. The chair of the spiritual athlete is neither higher nor lower than the chair of the sex addict. Both chairs manifest grandiose energies. You can be just as arrogant in the Mother Theresa mode as in the Madonna mode. Spiritual practice, then, can often be a clever disguise for someone possessed by infantile grandiosity and related delusional humility.

It is the genius and challenge of contemporary psychoanalytic theory to have given a comprehensive explanation of these things for the first time. We never before had such a powerful resource for discernment to help us realize that you must do more than identify with spiritual archetypes to be truly humble.

Audience: What would you say about the humility that Christ talked about? Or the renunciation that the Buddhists talk about, like being ego-less? Are they merely dreams?

Moore: To understand this you have to do a psychology of asceticism. Some early Christian literature did show Jesus giving a scathing critique of spiritual hypocrisy (Matthew, chapters 6 and 23), but nothing like a comprehensive understanding of its psychology. As for the spiritual realities in the actual life of Jesus, modern psychological studies tell us very little. We know enough to know that we don't know anything scientifically accurate about his personality. You have to entertain the possibility that modern interpretations of Christ and Buddha may be projections. We may still know something about Christ through faith, of course, relying on the written testimony of early Christians, but in terms of historical research, we know very little.

There is such a thing as humility, however, and we must learn the true humility that consists of two things: (a) knowing your limitations and (b) getting the help you need. That is all humility is. It has nothing to do with any ascetic personal style or with being self-effacing. It is simply knowing your limitations. That is what the grandiose self hates. The grandiose self does not want to know any limits, and it does not want to ask for help. The twelve-step programs are so powerful because they teach a form of humility that says: "Know your limitations, and get the help you need."

To return to our main topic, how does it feed psychological, pathological narcissism when we declare the entire sacred world nonexistent?

Audience: You would get all your gratification and fulfillment in the profane world through some kind of physical gratification?

Moore: So everything becomes unconsciously sacramental in a very shadowy way. You do not do away with sacraments. Humans cannot do away with sacraments, or sacrifice, or ritual. You just become unconscious and act it out. You become very literalistic. Instead of an offering from another world, as in the Christian myth, that comes into this world to feed you, you feed on others. There is still sacrifice, but you eat other people. This is the dynamic behind the vampire myth and psychological cannibalism.

In all the cities of the world today, the more our secularization has increased, the more we are "eating the children." Right as I speak here in River City, there are children being "eaten." Very few seem to care about these child prostitutes in Chicago, not to speak of the adult ones who are also being "eaten" by the spiritually hungry. The traffic in prostitution is an acted out, unconscious, ritualized sacrificial sacrament.

American intellectuals tend to ignore such things as this. We seldom worry about the prostitutes. You seldom hear anyone expressing any concern about them. A handful of people at Genesis House here in Chicago care about them, but it is hard for them to raise money. If you are a psychotherapist, you may have worked with some of the very people who are eating them, psychically and physically. It is so horrible that we cannot even let ourselves know that these children die very quickly. The life expectancy of prostitutes is not very high. I am not talking about Bangkok, and I am not talking about Bombay. Not long ago I drove down a street in Bombay where thousands of young women were lined up who had been sold into prostitution. At that time I was blind to the situation in Chicago and New York City, but later I learned how widespread it is.

We still engage in demonic sacramental behaviors, and terrible things happen when we don't have a conscious connection with the mythic realm, or as Robert Bly would say, the "other world." Robert Bly (1990) would say to a group of men: if you are not in touch with the king in the other world, your life in this world is going to be a terrible mess. I was surprised that we agreed on this.

Whether or not you believe these ideas theologically, or ontologically, or metaphysically, you better have some connection with them in a mythical sense. Myth needs to live for you, because if you do not have an "other world" where the gods and goddesses live, or a king and queen, then you are going to be eaten up with grandiose energies. You will either identify with the royal archetypes or project them onto other humans. Both paths lead to chaos.

From a Jungian point of view, I would argue, I should not try to tell you which myth to use to contain your archetypal projections, but only that you need conscious mythic and ritual containers. If you come to me for analysis and therapy, and you absolutely refuse to have any spirituality, I will still work with you, but I will have to tell you honestly that without a spiritual practice it will be much more difficult, perhaps impossible, for you to deal effectively with your archetypal Self, its grandiose energies, and its unconscious projections.

If you come into analysis with me without a spiritual life, you might project your god-complex onto me if you like me and idealize me. I will probably try to carry it, and we will be tempted to have one of those Woody Allen, twenty-year analyses. This is what happens with Freudians and other therapists who do not understand that an idealizing transference of the god-complex onto the therapist is a mythic and spiritual phenomenon. If a therapist has trouble letting people terminate their therapy, it is because it is not therapy, but unconscious religion. The therapist has become a little Holy Father with his own little pseudo-religion. "Worship me and bring me your sacrifices, and I will do my best to make it sacrificial for you. If I can talk you into the necessity of it, you will come to see me five times a week. If I belong to a certain school of thought, you may come to me for as long as twenty years."

When you terminate, however, you are likely to get depressed again. You will wonder what happened to all the money you spent on your analysis, because it's over now, but you're depressed again. You go consult someone else about it, and they tell you that obviously your analysis was not finished. I am not joking. Thousands of people have been in therapy forever, and they cannot understand why it does not work. Are they just particularly stupid in choosing therapists? Maybe, but the therapeutic process can also be undermined by the analyst's inferior theoretical understanding.

This underscores the importance of Jungian thought. Authentic Jungians are clear that you have to deal with an archetypal god-complex in your psyche. The archetypal psychologists and post-Jungian theorists who have no archetypal Self find it difficult to understand the psychological structure of a god-imago. If it possesses your ego, how would you be able to detect its grandiosity? If you identify with your god-imago, if it intrudes into your ego consciousness, you will get a narcissistic personality disorder, and your religion will be having everyone else adore you. Narcissistic people always try to find a dependent partner, so they can keep this private pseudo-religion going on in their image. They project their god-complex onto you, and get you to say, "Thank you, that is entirely appropriate." Millions of marriages are private pseudo-religions like that. They work fine until it begins to occur to the woman that she probably could find a better deity than this one if she tried. That is what happens when a woman gets started in therapy and then begins to realize that she might be able to accomplish the same thing somewhere else somewhat less expensively!

SUMMARY

We now have enough understanding available to us from psychoanalytic research to form an integrated understanding of the human spiritual problem. Eliade alone is not enough, Campbell alone is not enough, and Jung alone is not enough, but all their contributions work together to articulate a realization that the secularizing processes of modernity have not lessened the pathological narcissism and compulsive acting out of grandiose energies. As Jung saw clearly, the flooding of grandiose energies has increased to epidemic proportions.

Joseph Campbell has become so popular because people intuit their need to rediscover the mythic realm to deal with these energies. Why is that? Why must we rediscover the mythic realm? Because if we do not, our inner grandiose self organization will remain trapped in the human realm and cause us endless problems. *To deal with pathological grandiosity successfully, you must project it outside the human realm, and that is the function of myth.* If the full numinosity of the god-energy stays inside human relationships, Armageddon is upon us. We must get the numinous energy contained outside the realm of everyday life. The indigenous tribes understood this, and they were ahead of us on this. That is the meaning of the first commandment, "Thou shalt have no other gods before me." You may not believe it theologically, but it is still true psychologically.

Our contemporary challenge, then, is to rediscover ways to use ritual process and mythic vessels to contain and channel grandiose "god-energies." We can do this in a conscious way informed by these new psychoanalytic insights. Our forebears, lacking such insight, used myth and ritual to displace their grandiose energies onto their various tribal groups. They had no way of knowing that it was a bogus solution to achieve personal humility by displacing grandiosity onto the tribe, the royal personage, or the national identity. Social displacement of grandiosity still leaves the grandiose energies intact and fundamentally unchallenged. They have, in effect, gone underground and achieved social and even spiritual camouflage and sanction.

This kind of failed social displacement mechanism has been the engine behind all genocides, all racism, classism, sexism, nationalistic hubris, and religious and ideological warfare.[3] Rather than facing the dragon of our grandiosity consciously, the social displacement mechanisms have enabled the dragon to wreak havoc on our planet. Periodically, in families, communities, and in larger groups, the pressure of grandiose energies builds to intolerable levels, and people turn to desperate unconscious pseudo-ritualizations expressed in ritual violence that includes warfare and the quest for the human sacrifice of those weak enough to serve as scapegoats. Violent catharsis may lower the pressure for a while, but soon the dragon, cloaked in the darkness of unconsciousness, returns to feed its terrible insatiable appetite.[4]

Our challenge includes going beyond unconscious displacement techniques, ritual violence, and the use of scapegoats as unconscious means of controlling our grandiosity and its demonic consequences. We must face the dragon consciously with our new psychoanalytic knowledge. This presents a huge and decisive challenge for our species. Meeting it successfully can bring us to a new phase of human evolution, but ignoring it means we would rather continue arranging unconsciously for our own last rites.

NOTES

1. This chapter is an edited account of the late morning session on Saturday, July 15, 1989, of a weekend workshop and discussion led by Robert Moore at the C. G. Jung Institute in Chicago, Illinois. The original program was entitled "Jungian Psychology and Human Spirituality: Liberation from Tribalism in Religious Life."
2. My taped lectures, "Archetype, Compulsion, and Healing," are available from the C. G. Jung Institute of Chicago.
3. It is the sinister engine behind both the Enron debacle and the devastating events of September 11, 2001.
4. These psychodynamics of grandiosity underlie the ritual violence described in Gil Baillie, *Violence Unveiled* (1995).

Woman at Risk

CHAPTER 5

Discerning and Facing
Your Own Grandiosity

I F WE BUILD ON JUNG'S ORIGINAL VISION, JUNGIAN THOUGHT
is not just another point of view in the spectrum of theories. It is not just another esoteric cult for a few eccentric
mystics. A serious Jungian researcher does a lot of work in comparative mythology and comparative folklore in order to look for
the deep structures of the collective unconscious that are human
and not just tribal.[1] This makes the present time very important
when contrasted with previous eras in history, because scholars
have now provided us with access to enormous resources of comparative mythology never available before, much of it not available
to Jung himself. This new wealth of material creates an important
opportunity for enlarging human understanding. Jungians have
the special task of helping people find the continuities between all
this cross-cultural mythology and the many issues of human healing raised in comparative psychotherapy.

The image of the Tower of Babel relates directly to the issues of
this book. History since early tribalism has been a sort of rush
hour for the tribes. In the early days you could live in the rain for-
est and never meet anyone from another tribe. Later, as population
increased, you began to have intertribal conflicts that increased in
severity as the world became more crowded with tribes. The Tower

of Babel story portrays many different people talking in their own language, but no one understands what anyone else is saying. It is a revealing image of modern tribal conflict, but it also gives us an image of personality fragmentation. It symbolizes what happens in the psyche of a person who is very ill narcissistically.

The word *fragmentation* is a key technical term in contemporary psychoanalysis. We talk a lot today about "multiple personality disorder," but it is nothing new. It is simply the latest fad in talking about fragmentation and splitting in the psyche along archetypal lines. It is simply another way of talking about *autonomous complexes* that Jung was researching in the first decade of the twentieth century.[2] There is no new psychology of multiple personalities, but some non-Jungians have begun to pay attention to autonomous complexes. An autonomous complex is autonomous to the extent that it is unconscious and the psyche is being fragmented by its grandiose energies.

People suffering from a multiple personality disorder have not learned how to manage the grandiose energies in their personality. Just as you can understand addictions in terms of the psychology of pathological infantile grandiosity, so also can you understand multiple personality disorders. Whether in the individual psyche or the larger human community, when pathological infantile grandiosity invades, everything splits. The center cannot hold. Fragmentation occurs into different centers of organization. That is a human rule. It is fascinating how the biblical image of the Tower of Babel anticipates contemporary psychoanalytic theory in a rich and powerful way.

Audience: Is there a distinction between a narcissistic person and a borderline personality?

Moore: Yes. Everything is on a continuum developmentally from the most chaotic to the most highly integrated. The borderline personality is more integrated than a schizophrenic or a psychotic, but less integrated than a narcissistic personality disorder. We use this kind of language in two different ways. There is a particular diagnostic category in the psychiatric *Diagnostic and Statistical Manual of Mental Disorders* called "narcissistic personality disorder," but that is only one kind of disorder, the person who has identified with the god-complex but still manages not to be psychotic.

We all have to deal with narcissistic pathology, but for the borderline personality, the narcissistic pathology manifests itself in a more radical instability. If you happen to think that you are the king or queen of the universe and you are very gifted, you may become a surgeon or a judge, because you display such a genuine talent that people will let you get away with it. In fact, there are many roles in society where a narcissistic personality disorder can function because personal gifts can be tailored and grandiose energies channeled to achieve excellent performance in many different jobs and careers, and in many different social roles.

If you are not a very gifted person, however, it does not work so well. It is useless to tell people that they can become brain surgeons when they cannot read. What does such a person do in our society? You can always turn to crime. You can deal drugs. There are many of these people who make lots of money for a time as drug dealers. All they need is an automatic weapon and a willingness to serve the forces of death.

A borderline personality, however, is different. If you think you are the king and you have enough talent that people treat you like the king, then you do not get psychotic, because a certain structural stability is maintained. Given enough talent and public acceptance, you can maintain enormous psychological inflation without becoming psychotic. If you are gifted, people will often transfer their idealizing projections onto you, and you agree with them. "I am wonderful, and you are nothing." As long as people will accept you absolutely as God and they are just nothing, you will not be psychotic because you do not have to deal with your grandiosity. You have a social vessel for holding your grandiosity. You will not become psychotic because you have institutionalized the grandiosity into a social ritual where you can act like a complete jackass and people will just say, "Thank you! Thank you!"

Audience: It is not just toleration.

Moore: That is right. The masochistic position is just as inflated as the sadistic position. In a symbiotic partnership, we manage for both of us to be crazy without either one of us going psychotic. If you stop your end of the partnership, what will happen to me? I will get very crazy. If you stop your masochistic end of the partnership, then I will be threatened with psychosis.

The borderline personality differs in not being identified with the king or queen. Borderlines know that they are not the king or queen, but they also know that you are not either. Borderlines cannot find the king or queen, which means they have difficulty forming a stable idealizing transference. The life of a borderline consists of wandering around the world in search of a king or queen, because the king or queen is at the necessary center. They search for a vessel to contain their god-complex, but with little hope.

On the other hand, the borderline is very smart. Let me put it delicately and technically: their inner trickster works very well. That is why therapists hate to work with borderlines, because a borderline can see right through them. A borderline personality will not automatically see you as Mr. Wonderful or Ms. Wonderful. A lot of therapists do not want to face this. They don't like to treat borderlines because borderlines can see the negative truth about them. They will look at the therapist and say, "You don't really care about me," and often they are right. The borderline's intuition is sometimes so accurate that the therapist's denial of the accusation doesn't work. They experience the therapist as a shadow magician who doesn't care about them.

Therapists in their own grandiosity often display a narcissistic personality disorder. No one can stand criticism less than a grandiose therapist. It becomes countertransference when the analysand looks at the therapist and doesn't see a king or queen, and the therapist responds negatively by concluding that the analysand is a case of borderline personality. Here is how it works. The analysand thinks, "This therapist is bored with me and doesn't care about me." The analysand doesn't mirror the therapist by thinking, "This is my great and wonderful therapist, her Majesty the Therapist." The therapist picks up on that attitude and decides, "This analysand is sicker than I thought," and makes a diagnosis of borderline personality disorder, even though the interaction may simply reflect the analyst's own incompetence or bad faith.

A recent conference that I attended with Goldberg and Basch, the leading Chicago self psychologists, made this clear. Whether someone gets diagnosed borderline or not often depends more on whether the therapist can manage to have an empathic connection with them. If you come to me for therapy, and I am too narcissistic to attune to you and your needs, then I am more likely to diagnose you as borderline. But if you come to me and mirror me and make me feel good enough about myself as a therapist, then I may be able to like you enough for us to "make a connection," and you will feel attuned to me. Then, of course, I will know that you are *not* a borderline and, because you are treatable, I can diagnose you as a healthier person, one with another personality disorder rather than the more difficult borderline personality (see Basch 1988, 1992).

Audience: Does the term *borderline* mean the borderline of something?

Moore: The designation used to be called "borderline psychotic." It referred to a person who tended to be unstable but not as unstable and chaotic as a multiple personality or schizophrenic. That means archetypally that the person does not feel connected with the center, the *axis mundi* that is the locus of the thrones of the archetypal king and queen. Many primitive mythologies have two thrones. Whose thrones are they? The king's throne and the queen's throne. In patriarchy, of course, you get a king, and people can't figure out what that other throne is for! Why does Pharaoh sit on two thrones? This is not true in later developments, but the archetypal realm always has two thrones.

We have these thrones at the *axis mundi*, but people are still searching for a connection to those thrones if they have no spiritual life, or do not believe in God, or do not otherwise participate consciously in myth. Remember, this is not religion, this is psychology. You are looking for a place to put that grandiose projection. So we put the analyst's chair over here for a throne, and I become your Freudian psychoanalyst, and you become my analysand, and you can worship me for as long as you like, five days a week. You may have such severe narcissistic pathology that you are never able to terminate the relationship. You may see me for twenty years or more and still not be healed. "I really am sorry that you are so sick. Your mother was so bad. It is all her fault."

This is usually not an intentional cynicism on the part of the psychoanalyst, but some of the most destructive people in the world meant well. When your therapist, whether Jungian, Freudian, Adlerian, Rogerian, behaviorist, cognitive, or whatever, unconsciously accepts your god transference and laments how crazy you are and how wonderful it is that you have found him, you have just managed to find a way to deal with your need for archetypal transference of the king and queen.

As long as your analyst carries your archetypal transference for you and is not aware that you need to be dealing with it in some other way as soon as you can, then your situation is interminable "analysis." You may quit therapy, perhaps because you get sick of paying, but then an interesting thing happens. What happens if you quit therapy before you find a spiritual solution to your problems?

Audience: You go find yourself another therapist?

Moore: Yes, you can find another therapist, or what?

Audience: You become psychotic?

Moore: Yes, you may become psychotic, but at the very least you get sick again. There are many forms this sickness can take.[3] What are some of the forms it can take? Suppose that I have been in therapy with you for six years, and in my relationship with you, I have gotten so much better that I no longer have any large symptoms. I am not acting out, I am not overeating, I am not into compulsive drinking, or any other kind of compulsive behavior. So I quit my therapy, but all of a sudden I go back on the sauce, start drinking again, more heavily perhaps, or I gain thirty pounds, or sexually I start acting out promiscuously, or I get a divorce and remarry. All because of what?

I have not taken my archetypal transference – my projection of grandiose energies – off of you, my therapist who had become my false center. I had put my Aphrodite goddess transference onto you, and though you would not have sex with me because you knew you might get sued, I put onto you all the goddess transference I had to give. That made you magical and wonderful, and I felt so wonderful in this relationship with you. My wife looks at me, and she is always criticizing me, and she does not always think that I am so wonderful. She thinks I did not balance my checkbook, or I did not take out the garbage. So I do not feel so good with my wife, but with you, my therapist, I feel whole again. Now I know that what I needed after all was not therapy. What I needed was you. Maybe I can talk you into a divorce and marry you. But just as soon as I marry you, you will not be able to contain my idealization any better than my ex-wife did, and soon you will start looking just like her. I thought I got away from her, but I find out that I did not get away from her. This can go on and on.

It continues to work this way until finally I figure it out and realize I have a problem. I probably need to go back to school, get another degree, become more wonderful! Then everything will be all right again. Almost everyone can elaborate on this from their own experience. If we had enough time, we could look at all the various ways an analysand might act out after leaving this kind of therapy. I may think that I could not internalize anything when I was working with you. It was all there in you. You were the god or the goddess, or I probably projected both sides of the Godhead onto you. The psychoanalytic self psychologists make it clear that as long as I am in a satisfactory selfobject transference with you, I will often not have any symptoms. Why not? Because I am containing my grandiosity in you. It is often called a "transference cure," but it is no cure at all.

The analysand's grandiosity is contained in the analyst who serves as god or goddess or both, while the analysand, by contrast, is nothing. I am much better when I am with this analyst, but why? Someone tell me why I am better when I am with her.

Audience: It is a symbiotic relationship.

Moore: Symbiotic, that is absolutely right, but it is not just that it is symbiotic. It is more subtle than that. There is some specific thing happening here. I am putting something into her. I am putting a projection onto her or into her, but what is the content of that projection? This is the genius of Jungian thought. Freudians are good phenomenologists who see a lot of this micro-plumbing better than Jungians do, but they do not understand the nature of the content as well as Jungians do. I am putting a specific content into her. It is an aspect or sector of the god-imago.

Audience: It is embodied in the relationship.

Moore: It is unconsciously contained in the relationship. You want to think "containment" because it relates to ritual. It is embodied in this, but it is in the field. It is in the relationship. As long as I have my relationship with you, I will not be as crazy in my behavior. My acting out will be limited.

Audience: What about a negative transference?

Moore: It depends on how severe the negative transference is. If I come to see you and it is not very good, then I may have difficulty projecting an archetypal transference onto you in spite of any longings I may have. That is not an archetypal negative transference. It is ordinary. You are just ordinarily uninteresting as a therapist. When I am with you, I do not feel very interesting myself. At least you are not interesting enough for me to pay your large fees, and that means I'll not be coming back to see you. I'm just checking out therapists anyway. I've seen four this month and not one of them has been all that interesting. What does that translate out as? No archetypal transference is occurring despite my archetypal longings.

On the other hand, suppose that when I first come to see you, the moment I come into your office I know that you are the therapist I need to see. When I visited all those other therapists, something told me they were not the right ones, but when I came in here with you, something told me that you were the answer. You are the person I need to work with. I have a positive archetypal transference and you carry the light side of the god and the goddess for me. Everything is fine and dandy as long as you make me feel wonderful by blessing me with those beautiful eyes. Oh, I just feel so good when I am with you and you see and recognize me.

That lasts for a short time, and then one day I display my grandiosity to you in what we call a mirror transference. You will gaze upon me, and I will be the divine child in the manger, and I will ooh and ah and you will smile, and I will feel as if this were a crèche (the tableau of Mary, Joseph, and others around the crib of the baby Jesus in the Bethlehem stable, often built for Christmas display). Right here, this is a crèche. You (the analyst) are looking at me, and we have the cow, and the goat, and the shepherd and all, and the little squirrel up there, and you are all gazing at me (the analysand), and I just feel so wonderful displaying myself to you, and everything is fine as long as I am the Christ child in the crèche.

But then one day, you (the analyst) stayed out too late the night before or you are preoccupied, and you do not manage to mirror me (the analysand) quite adequately. Suddenly it becomes clear to me that I was mistaken. You (the analyst) are not Mary at all like I thought you were. You are really Lilith (a female demon in ancient Near Eastern literature) or, if you are a male, you are really Satan. Now I see that you are just in this for the money, that you are just exploiting me. Now you are not just uninteresting, which means no archetypal transference at all, but you are evil. That is the archetypal satanic transference.

Audience: Do not self psychologists say that the mirroring is the healing? Then what does the process of the rupture represent?

Moore: It depends on why it occurred. If the analysand walks out of the room and never comes back, the self psychologists do not think that healing occurred at all. Why?

Audience: Well, right, you are not there, there is no holding.

Moore: There is no holding, and therefore the analyst cannot take the analysand down off the throne a little bit in a process of slow de-idealization. It cannot be done later, because the analyst really seems like Satan to the analysand. Here the analysand attacks the therapist for being a female version of Satan, and she may surprise the analysand by saying, "Just get out of here! I do not have to put up with this abuse!" All the analysand can do is just get away. Even if the analyst thinks, "No, I am not Satan or

Lilith, you are just a borderline personality," which is, in effect, what a lot of therapists do, then there will probably be a breach. Many therapists cannot endure such an attack. They retaliate against the analysand and effectively terminate them right there. It is much more common than cases of therapists who can contain an attack.

Suppose, on the other hand, that the analyst says, "You must have really felt betrayed by me." Now the analysand says, "What's this?! This Satan is worrying that she might have betrayed me?!" That kind of empathic response confuses the analysand who was expecting a negative response.

Then the analyst says, "I hope at least that you will come back next Monday and let's talk about what just happened between us, because I think I understand something about how you are feeling now, and what I have done to disappoint you." The phrase "What I have done to disappoint you" is just a euphemistic way of admitting "I have failed you."

What has changed in psychotherapy today is that it has become acceptable for therapists to admit that they are not always totally empathic. This makes it harder for the analysand to think that the disappointing analyst really is Satan. "It once felt wonderful when we were attuned, but today I feel terrible and I don't feel good around you anymore. I can't be sure that you are Satan, though, so I will come back next time and see what happens." When the analyst can adequately interpret the break in empathy so that it feels accurate to the analysand, it may allow a new opportunity for healing to occur.

Audience: What, then, is the role of the therapist. You say that all this transference of archetypal contents is an important human and natural part of therapy, but you also seem to say it is inappropriate for the therapeutic process.

Moore: No, no, I think it is a necessary part of the process.

Audience: In terms of spirituality, what is the relevance of all the conflict and different frames of reference of Freudian or self psychology? How does the spiritual aspect fit into all this?

Moore: When self psychologists discuss mirroring and idealizing transference, they do not realize they are talking about the management of archetypal transference. It is possible to encounter these realities without knowing that they are archetypal. They talk about dealing with grandiosity, for example, and they help analysands gradually become more and more capable of relating to their own grandiosity and being much more accepting of it because their therapist accepts it. Nonetheless, I think it is important to point out the weakness of any theory of psychotherapy that does not clearly understand the relationship between the archetypal Self and the ego, how this influences analysand-analyst relationships and how the archetypal projection must be removed from humans. The archetypal transference does not belong on human beings. The spiritual resources of the mythic imagination are required to cope adequately with these powerful archetypal energies.

Audience: So you are saying that many therapists remove the projection from themselves and put it back in the context of the analysand's personal life, and the problem is not whether transference and idealization exist, but that they don't separate the sacred and the profane world within their analysands. They take the analysand's idealizing projection, and the analysand is left with a sort of existential loss. So do you mean that the problem is not in the psychological structure of the projection, but in the placing of it in the physical environment?

Moore: Yes, from my point of view, there can be no adequate termination until you find an appropriate vessel for an archetypal transference, but that vessel must not be human. It was the genius of Eliade to see that, but he did not have a psychology to explain it. He leaned heavily toward the Jungian viewpoint, but he could never admit it publicly, because in his university it was never acceptable to be Jungian. It still isn't to this day at the University of Chicago.

Audience: So what would that container be?

Moore: There are many different mythic forms in human history, and from a psychological point of view, you would not prescribe which myth would be most helpful to carry it. Jung would say if you can go to church, then go to church, because he thought many people could get this archetypal transference carried by a traditional religious form. From a psychological point of view, you cannot prescribe what is "the right myth," but you can urge development of an ego-Self axis of separation between your ego and the archetypal Self which is the transpersonal, transegoic center in the psyche.[4]

It will work psychologically for an individual to project and displace the grandiose energies onto a human ideology. If you become an ideologue, it does not matter psychologically whether you are a Reaganite or a Marxist, so long as the ideology is numinous for you. Psychodynamically speaking, if an ideology becomes the carrier for your archetypal Self, it will keep you from fragmenting as an individual in a way similar to how you seemed to get better through transference to a therapist. The ideology serves as a psychological prosthesis for the individual while the grandiosity continues having a toxic effect at the cultural and societal level.

That is what happens in malignant human tribalism. You can view human religious tribalism or ethnicity in these terms. When your ethnic, or racial, or religious group become numinous for you as an individual, the group will carry the numinosity of your archetypal Self. That will protect your ego from the grandiosity, but it will not protect other people or the world from it. Note the devastation that has resulted from the numinosity of Marxist ideology.

Audience: Related to my other question about renunciation in Buddhism and Christianity, if one becomes too sacred in relating to the Self, doesn't an imbalance occur in mortification and asceticism? Don't you need a middle ground? Would you comment on that?

Moore: When you get into one of these holy configurations, archetypal energy invades the ego from that part of the archetypal Self that is shaped like a monk, but other archetypal structures look very different. The warrior aspect is one form that this asceticism can take. The monk is often a spiritual warrior who combines aspects of both the magician and warrior archetypes. It may look ascetic and selfless even when it is very inflated. Your grandiose energies can flow through various structures that glow with their own unique patterns of archetypal energy. You may not consider them inflated, but they are.[5]

You can also take the grandiosity off your ego through different forms of tribalism to keep it from fragmenting. "I am not psychotic if I can project my grandiosity onto something else. If I project it onto you, you might become psychotic, but not me!" This is something you see in therapy a lot. In short, we appear to be more integrated than we really are.

A lot of therapists, when they carry the archetypal transferences of other people, find themselves having disturbing symptoms. They might say, "I've had twenty years of therapy, and I feel just as crazy as I did when I started." What they don't realize is that other people's archetypal transferences have overstimulated their own grandiosity. When people turn you into a god or goddess, it tends to make you more crazy, not less. They say, "I can get rid of my god-complex by putting it on my therapist," but then the therapist has the archetypal energies of two god-complexes to contend with, his and theirs, which makes it doubly hard for the therapist to keep an integrated personality.

In this light, we can see that clergy of all faiths have very dangerous jobs. On Sunday morning, for example, when the priest gets up there, if he is a good liturgist, he will elicit archetypal transference (see Randall 1988). On the other hand, if he is not good at it, the people in the audience will not experience archetypal transference. When the priest has a true talent for liturgy, what Victor Turner called "ritual genius," archetypal transference will often occur. This is fine for the congregation, because it passes all its transferences over to the priest, but the priest now has to deal with them, and this can tremendously overstimulate his own grandiose self-organization. He may feel enormous anxiety and go get himself a drink. That is why there are so many alcoholic and pedophile priests. They have to self-medicate to deal with the overstimulation coming from all the archetypal transferences from the people.

Substance abuse and sexual addictions are pseudo-ritualizations that people use to regulate their grandiose energies. It is not just psychotherapists who have this problem. In fact, it is harder for clergy, because they may have dozens or hundreds of people in the same room projecting upon them at the same time, while therapists only have one analysand in the room at a time to deal with.

Audience: What is it that makes a narcissistic grandiose person fragment?

Moore: The human ego cannot contain God.

Audience: But if the human ego sees itself as God, wouldn't that be a substitute? Couldn't the human self-inflated ego be a substitute for God, psychologically speaking?

Moore: It seems to approach that with some people. The narcissistic personality disorder is sometimes able to entertain a godlike fantasy because of certain ritualizations with certain other people who are comfortable enough with it not to cause psychosis. Nonetheless, on the other side of it, the narcissistic personality disorder can still have severe symptoms that are not psychotic. You may be identifying with the god-complex, but not so far out as to be psychotic, yet still enough to have significant symptoms.

Whenever a person has that kind of delusional inflation, they will always experience symptoms that are trying to say, "Hey, you're still human, and don't forget that you are human." What kind of symptoms? Perhaps they will masturbate compulsively, or look at pornography a lot. In fact, they may have a whole suitcase of pornography that they take with them, because they identify so strongly with the god-complex that they fear they will become disembodied or lose their humanity by losing their body. Sometimes they will not understand what the symptoms are, but they will notice that they have to masturbate, sometimes ten times a day. Why would anyone have to masturbate that much?

Audience: The pain is so great.

There is so much anxiety.

To get balance with your body physically.

Moore: You must get in touch with your body! The dragon in you is trying to get you to forget that you are human, so you masturbate to make sure you stay in touch with your body. You stay embodied that way.

This is obviously a different view of masturbation. In a lecture to some conservative Christians the other night, I was talking about prayer, and I said that prayer was this, and prayer was that, but when I got to the idea of "masturbation as prayer," that raised some eyebrows! But this is serious. Part of you knows that you are unaware that you are not God, and masturbation is a compulsive physical way of reminding you that you are human after all.

Audience: We see that with Jimmy Swaggart and Jim Baker.

Moore: One could argue that Jimmy gets so inflated into the messianic king that he needs to get clear with this prostitute that he is only a man after all. The messianic king in the psyche is an archetypal king-warrior with no interest in sex. The king is too busy for sex. Then, out of all the archetypal possibilities, the king's shadow arrives as the archetypal lover, and all of a sudden you get something that counters this particular king inflation, and he turns his back on his work as king to look at this woman. Very much like a man.

Audience: What about the Zeus complex? You get the Gary Harts of the world.

Moore: Yes, and you see it in J. F. K. and other powerful men who get so many idealizing projections that they are overwhelmed with grandiose energies.

Audience: A priest who has all these projections of everyone else's god-complex and is overstimulated and wants to drink to deal with it but says, "I don't want to drink because I'm a priest," what can he do?

Moore: That is where the issue of spirituality comes in. A lot of people think prayer is something only spiritual athletes do, as if prayer were the esoteric fifteenth initiation, but if you really understand it, prayer is a survival technique. If you are in one of these helping professions where you get a lot of archetypal transferences, you do not pray because it is pious or sweet or nice or the fifteenth initiation. You pray to stay alive, to get help in dealing with your grandiosity. I gave a lecture this past week in North Carolina entitled "Prayer as Survival Technique" to deal with grandiosity. Prayer is one of the greatest antidotes to being flooded with the grandiose numinous energies of other people.

If you cannot pray, if you do not pray a lot and you do not have a sense of how to pass on the numinous energy to a mythic vessel, you need to learn how. You can take that energy that is coming toward you and, through your prayer, pass it on. "Here," you say, "this is really yours, Lord. Take it. It belongs to you." If you keep it within yourself, you will soon be drunk with archetypal energies.

Prayer is a process of passing on the numinous magical god-energy. (Chapter 10 examines prayer in more detail.)

My basic argument is simply that humans need to get rid of the overload on their psychic circuits. There is a certain amount of this energy that you want to be connected with. It is a connection, not a separation. We do not want to lose touch with this energy because it is like an umbilical cord. It is a life-giving, nourishing connection with the libido for life. If you cut the connection, you will invariably get severely depressed. Your self-esteem will be lousy. Without a conscious connection to the archetypal Self, your ego's life becomes extremely impoverished. You can never get rid of the archetypal Self because it becomes more compulsively active the more you are unconscious of it.

Without a good conscious connection with the archetypal Self, you deny it and split it off, and it goes into the shadow and gets you into trouble. You get depressed, your self-esteem goes down, you don't think you are important, and you don't take yourself seriously. You don't believe you are significant enough to do anything significant. You don't think you are beautiful enough to be loved. If someone comes into your life who wants to love you, you push them away because you have no sense of your own beauty. These are very subtle but powerful forces.

It is like refueling a jet fighter from the big mother plane. Did you ever see pictures of that? They come up above you and have this boom hanging down, and they have to be careful when they plug in. You don't want to merge with the mother plane! It would be a fireball, right? But if you don't plug in for the refueling, you will soon run out of fuel. You have to be careful about that connection. That is the hard part.

That is spirituality. Human spirituality, psychodynamically speaking, is being able to connect with the refueling source without crashing into it. This is the ego-archetypal Self axis.

Audience: Is that another way of saying what Joseph Campbell means when he says to just "follow your bliss"?

Moore: It is more than that, but "follow your bliss" assumes that you have the potential for joy, and if you do not have joy, you are flying too low. You have to fly up a little closer and get your nozzle into the receptacle, because it is your birthright as a human being to experience joy. In that sense, "follow your bliss" is good advice.

Campbell's main contribution, however, was to show us the richness of world mythology as a resource for understanding the archetypal realm and also for understanding the dangers involved in relating to it. His book *The Hero with a Thousand Faces* (1949) is a little manual on relating to the archetypal energies. The hero journeys deep down into the underworld to get the boon, the gift, the numinous energy, but you always have to come back to the human world. It is one thing to connect with the archetypal energy, but it is another thing to get back to being human. Here is your choice. You can stay at the surface and not seek connection with the god-energy, or you can go down and make connection but get so inflated that you are destroyed before you can get back out to the everyday world.

Campbell's work explains what world mythology says about all this. This includes every mythology, every mythic world, not just the Christian tradition. Human beings before the modern era understood these things. The modern world has forgotten how all this works and turned instead to the idea that we can strip-mine this territory. We expect to go in there and get some of that god-energy by strip-mining. This is the heroic modern ego trying to take control of it. We think that we do not have time to make long heroic journeys down into the god-energy and then come back again. We turn spirituality into a West Virginia coal mine, and our fantasy is that we can just mine all this god-energy whenever we need it and then we can manipulate it. It does not work except as a contemporary expression of demonic sorcery.

Audience: How does a shaman relate to the problems you described for priests?

Moore: This is not to disparage your question, but shamans make all the same mistakes as priests. It is all the same problem, no matter what tribe you are in. A lot of people think, "Ah, I went on a vision quest and now I'm a shaman," but these self-proclaimed shamans are just as inflated as "individuated analysts." A shaman is just one little subcultural form of magician that exists in every culture, whether they are called Baptist preachers, Pentecostal preachers like Swaggart, or Japanese Zen masters, or North American Indian shamans. They all have the same strengths and weaknesses. As for the ones who come and tell you that they have already found what you are looking for, if they are serious, what they have found is an inflated personality, a magician inflation.

Remember, there is no such thing as a person who has completely transformed his or her own narcissism. There are only people who acknowledge the existence of their grandiose energies and try to learn how to relate to them consciously and regulate and optimize their contacts with them intelligently.

Audience: Does not Eliade make the same distinction between the shaman and the psychotic, because the shaman can come back at will?

Moore: Yes, absolutely, but he is talking about the true shaman. It would be the same thing with the true priest, or the true clergyman, anyone who can touch the god-energy, the numinous, and, because of their spiritual practice and wisdom, not be seduced or destroyed by it. When you touch the numinous without the wisdom to regulate the grandiosity, it blows you up like the cartoons of the person who cannot get off the air-hose, so they inflate like a big balloon and float away.

Audience: Like the Monty Python image where the person ate and ate until they exploded?

Moore: That's exactly what it's like. It was Jung's genius to see that all this is not cultural but in the hard wiring. This is the *collective unconscious,* a concept of enormous significance. All humans are alike at this level. Inside we are all plugged into the numinous. We all have the life-or-death problem of learning how to develop an adequate connection to it, one that can fill us up into our full humanity. This is a lot more wonderful than many people think. If you are really plugged into that, the archetypal Self is able to fill you out so that you are fully inflated like a basketball. People who regulate and optimize contact with these energies often become quite awesome.

Most people are not narcissistic personality disorders in the classical sense. They are not too full of themselves but more like basketballs without enough air in them. You bounce them and they are a little flat. That is not true if you are really in touch with the "Great Self Within." That is the genius of the Christian *imago Dei* and the idea of the "mark of David." Everyone has the stamp of God, and it is a real likeness, a divine likeness. It is not identical with God, but it is the divine likeness, the divine spirit, the god-energy.

From a Jungian perspective, people plugged into that source of energy can "fill up" to the level that they were really designed for. How many pounds of pressure per square inch, I do not know, but when you are as full of yourself as you need to be to be fully human, you can be fantastic! This is where the Human Potential movement was right, and the humanistic psychologists were right.

But staying in the context of my assumptions, what was the problem with humanistic psychology?

Audience: They need the transpersonal.

Moore: They need the transpersonal dimension to deal with the excesses of narcissism.

Audience: Maslow did that in his own right, did he not?

Moore: Yes, but the point is to get in touch with a healthy narcissism. The word *narcissism* is no longer always a bad word in psychoanalysis. There is a healthy narcissism that results in self-esteem and a healthy exhibitionism, in contrast to pathological narcissism, which results in an oscillation between arrogance and terrible self-hate.

Audience: I am trying to understand archetypal experience. When people come up and tell the priest they think of him as God, is that a mental and verbal thing, or does it have more to do with the energy transfer from God?

Moore: Suppose, for example, that Jim here is a fine priest. He has his own issues, but he realizes that he is human and imperfect. Suppose further that I am very hungry when I come to where he is doing a Mass, and I need to have what self psychologists call "an idealizing transference." I need to idealize someone, because I feel so bad. I can't idealize myself, because I know what a jerk I am. To feel complete, I need to idealize someone in a self-object experience, so I idealize Jim the priest. This makes me feel better, so I go to Jim and say, "Father, you gave a wonderful homily today. It made me feel so good. I really felt united with Christ. You are so wonderful. I wish I could hear you do the homily every week."

If I don't mean it, then he'll know it, but it probably won't bother him and he'll be okay. But if I really do mean it, and particularly if I'm believable, the human Jim still may not deal with it much, but it might stimulate the grandiose Self inside. Going back repeatedly with this same wonderful message will continue to stimulate the grandiose self-organization in there, and he may not be able to protect himself from that. Your human ego may not buy flattery, but your grandiosity will. You cannot stop it. You cannot prevent me from getting through to your archetypal grandiosity. As far as I can tell, that is something that only the most sophisticated scholars of transference and countertransference understand.

Audience: Mothers know what it feels like. When a child idealizes you, you are "It." Their entire life depends on whether or not you care for them enough to feed them or allow them to do whatever it is they want to do, and they look at you with those eyes like, "Ah, yes!"

Moore: You are the goddess.

Audience: Right. I think many mothers feel it a lot and have a hard time managing it and giving it back, letting their kids say, "Oh, what a terrific mom!"

Moore: The Kohutian self psychology people in Chicago offer more on the nuts-and-bolts practical aspects of this than anyone else, much more than the Jungians do. The Jungians do not pay enough attention to this on a microdynamic level.

Audience: It is structure building, though, the accretion of structure, as opposed to the content.

Moore: That is right. It is extremely important to understand that we are all vulnerable to the overstimulation of this kind of idealization. Building the capacity to contain it and not identify with it is a big job. It takes lot of work. The more internal the structure, the more we can regulate grandiose energies.

Audience: Is not child abuse an attempt to deflate grandiosity and kill it? The parent just says, "I cannot live with that."

Moore: That is an important point. We have to make this idea more widespread, because otherwise we cannot understand the behaviors. When a parent attacks a child in this way, they are trying to deal with the very real issue of the grandiose energies in the child, though in a destructive way. They are responding to the real issue of their own shame at being deified. You have an involuntary shame response when someone idealizes you. You cannot stop. You cannot keep from having a shame response. It is auto-matic in most people.

Your shame response will differ depending on your familiarity with the psyche in these issues. Lashing out at the child is one way. There are all kinds of other forms of unconscious acting out that we do to make it clear that we are not the god or the goddess. That is a form of unconscious ritual and spirituality. The only problem is that most forms of unconscious spirituality, that is, clinging to the human and not being god, are usually destructive of self or others or both.

DEFENSES AGAINST GRANDIOSITY

Audience: I understand what you said about the parent's shame at being deified, and they would experience more of it the more they put themselves up to be worshipped. But why wouldn't they want that, and why would they react to it with shame? I don't under-stand.

Moore: We can look at the defenses against grandiosity. When your grandiose self organization, your archetypal Self, is overstim-ulated, you will try to defend against it because you instinctively know that it is not right. There is something wrong. You may not be able to write a Kohutian book on narcissism, or a Jungian book on the ego-Self axis, but you do not need to, because this is some-thing in the hardwiring. Something inside you knows there is something wrong with this psychological situation.

There are three kinds of defenses against overstimulated grandiosity. First, you can defend against grandiosity by just feel-ing overwhelmed by it and shutting down. It is one thing to have a little fun fantasy and think you are Batman. Not too many of us boys ever went through childhood without wanting to be Batman, but if you start thinking you really are Batman, or Batwoman, what happens is that now you have to take care of Gotham City. It is one thing to play like "Wouldn't it be nice to be Batman," but if I actually were Batman and I actually lived in Chicago, I would actually have to deal with all the drug dealers in Chicago. There is not enough time in Batman's life to do this.

So one defense against grandiosity results simply from feeling like the mythical hero Atlas who lost an important battle and was condemned to hold the earth on his shoulders for all eternity. You feel this enormous crushing weight of the grandiosity that you are experiencing, and you just cannot take it. It is just too much. This is another reason why the mother hits the kids, because sometimes even to acknowledge that she is your mother is overwhelming to her. So that is the first defense, the experience of being over-whelmed and the "shut down" that usually follows immediately.

The second defense against overstimulated grandiosity is a fear of shame and ridicule. You sense that someone is pointing their finger at you and saying, "You are getting too big for your britches!" You start remembering all those disappointing times in childhood. No telling how many thousands of times each one of us came running in with pure wonderfulness but were met by a bored or irritable response. Any time a child comes in wonderful like that and is not met with a positive response like, "Oh, wow, you really are feeling wonderful today!" then the sense of wonderfulness tends to collapse into shame and become locked in the unconscious.

We all carry enough shame in our unconscious from those early experiences that we do not want any more of that kind of ridicule. When you start feeling contact with your wonderfulness again, you are always in danger of this kind of toxic shame response taking over. Then you fear the ridicule, because of what happened to you in your childhood when you were really in touch with your radiance and it was squashed.

So the first defense against overstimulated grandiosity is to feel overwhelmed, and the second defense is to fear being ridiculed.

The third defense is interesting but different. Connection with your divine energies can rapidly become overstimulating. Even if it doesn't overwhelm you, and even if you feel no shame, it may provide you with too much stimulation, like a perpetual orgasm, and thus generate what we call "fragmentation anxiety." You can't cope with it because it makes you crazy, and it can rapidly morph into a prepsychotic state. You fear the psychosis that can come from the godlike intensity of too much energy flow from the archetypal Self. If you have ever been with someone who was in a manic phase or right on the edge of a manic phase, then you recognize this prepsychotic intensity. We say that they are wired. They have a certain look in the eyes, they are chain-smoking, or perhaps having a masturbation marathon. In the movie *The Right Stuff* (1983), they are flying right at the edge of the envelope, and it is so intense that it threatens fragmentation of the self structure and an incipient psychosis. To the extent that your ego structure, in Jungian terms, or your little "s" self, in Kohutian terms, is not fully reinforced, you may fear psychosis as a response to overstimulated grandiosity. This will often result in what we call a "panic attack," which recruits outside help in containing the archetypal energy.

Connection with your numinosity will not make you psychotic if you realize that you are a human being and not going to live forever, if you are oriented in the limitations of time and space, and if your self structure as a human is pretty firm. But to the extent that you are not well oriented in time, or not well oriented in gender, or not well oriented to much of anything, then it may not really be clear to you that you are going to die soon. You may feel as if you were bulletproof, and this increases your risk of a psychotic episode or acute depression, for you are channeling too much numinosity. Why depression? Because you must have the ballast, the heaviness of the depression to avoid a psychotic "flight into the sun," an expression of the Icarus complex.

So we have a number of unconscious ways to defend against being overwhelmed by our grandiose energies. Remember that according to Kohutian self psychology, grandiosity is not a bad thing in itself unless you do not manage it well so it fuels your ordinary life. The self psychologists are less judgmental about grandiosity. They want to help people relate to it consciously. I have heard a number of stories about people who were practicing from that point of view who helped people get their grandiosity under control. Self psychologists try to get the grandiose fantasies out in the open where you can see them and then help you find some way to relate to them and to embody them. They do not judge them. They help you get that energy connected to life. If the energy splits off, the grandiose fantasies get stuffed into the unconscious, one's life is impoverished, and symptoms begin to proliferate.

This parallels a Jungian point of view. We don't want to eliminate archetypal energies, but neither do we want them to destroy us. We want and need these energies to fuel and enrich life. That is the true meaning of human spirituality on the psychological level, to facilitate productive and creative contact with these sacred energies. That is why Jungians are uniquely able to diagnose grandiosity and the threat of pathological narcissism as spiritual problems that no one in the modern secular world can avoid having to deal with.

NOTES

1. This chapter is an edited account of part of the afternoon sessions on Saturday, July 15, 1989, of a weekend workshop and discussion led by Robert Moore at the C. G. Jung Institute in Chicago, Illinois. The original program was entitled "Jungian Psychology and Human Spirituality: Liberation from Tribalism in Religious Life."

2. Jung developed the concept of complexes before the period of his association with Freud 1907 to 1913. See Coan (1984).

3. See Robert L. Moore's audiotaped lectures, "The Collective Unconscious and Psychopathology" and "Archetype, Compulsion, and Healing," available from the C. G. Jung Institute of Chicago.

4. For a sophisticated discussion of the ego-Self axis, see Edward F. Edinger, *Ego and Archetype: Individuation and the Religious Function of the Psyche* (1972).

5. Robert L. Moore, audiotaped lecture, "Archetype, Compulsion, and Healing," available from the C. G. Jung Institute of Chicago.

CHAPTER 6

Decoding the Diamond Body

Archetypal Structures Provide a Framework for Analysis

THE SEARCH FOR DEEP STRUCTURES

This chapter presents an introduction to my decoding of the major archetypal structures in the inner geography of the psyche. It provides an important new framework for analyzing and understanding the forms through which grandiose energies manifest themselves in the human personality.[1]

Many complexities arise when trying to analyze how these phenomena of grandiosity and narcissism shape the personalities of different people struggling with various archetypal forces. My own research has given a great deal of attention to how one might model these diverse interactions in a comprehensive geometric code that extends Jung's own work on the topic.

Diagrams 1 through 4 in the appendix show the different structural configurations and lines of development indicated by my research on the archetypal Self. These configurations may be considered as inner spaces in dialectical tension. Depending on which archetypal configuration dominates the psyche, any one of four different kinds of space may open up.

Jung's studies of alchemy led him to believe that the archetypal

Self was imaged in what he called the *coniunctio*, the *mysterium coniunctionis*, the sacred marriage, the marriage of *rex* and *regina*, the king and the queen. I think he was right about that and more right than even he realized. Today we have much more comparative scholarly and general knowledge about world religion and mythology than existed in Jung's time. He was a great student of mythology, but since his time anthropology, comparative mythology, and the study of the history and phenomenology of religion have gone much further.[2]

Two good places to start are Jean Bolen's books, *Goddesses in Everywoman* (1984) and *Gods in Everyman* (1989). She worked mostly with Greek myths, however, and remember that even though *psyche* is a Greek word, the psyche itself is human, not just Greek! That means that we have to look at the comparative perspectives of Joseph Campbell, Mircea Eliade, and other comparative mythologists to broaden our data base. The fullness of the feminine and the masculine is much richer than we had realized before.

The reason Jung had some problems getting past Victorian stereotypes of the male and female psyches was thus partially informational. With access to more of the myths, he would have understood better, and many other classical Jungians would have understood better, that goddesses are good at some things other than being traditionally Victorian females. Jung's narrow view of masculinity and femininity was consistent with his times, for he tended to identify femininity with Victorian images of the feminine.

My own research has shown that the masculine and the feminine are much more complex than Jung and classical Jungians realized. The spectrum of the manifestation of both femininity and masculinity is more rich and balanced.

The goddess is not just identical to Mother Earth, and in fact, I think that idea is really a misreading. All this Gaia talk is nice, and I like it ecologically, but the goddess is not the earth to be walked on. She has capacities for domination and aggression as well. There is aggressive, agonistic femininity as well as passive, receptive femininity, and there is gentle, receptive, loving masculinity as well as aggressive, nonfeeling masculinity. The old classic Jungian idea that "man is Logos and woman Eros" is dated now and no longer adequate to our information.

My theory argues that world mythology contains eight basic images of male and female in their divine forms. My first geographic representation of this inner space naturally started where I myself was the most inflated, which as a therapist was in the magician area. Lee Roloff, one of our analysts here at the Jung Institute, has a saying that I think is so true, "In every re-search there is always a me-search."

In my first book (Moore 1979), I psychoanalyzed a priest, an inflated priest, John Wesley. Why? Because I had a lot of that in my own psyche, and I did not quite get it. I started doing a psychology of the occult and all the inflated magi. I spent ten years going around the United States doing field interviews with all kinds of occultists: ritual magicians, occult leaders, gurus, witches. It was really a personal quest trying to deal with my own magus inflation, but I did not know that at the time, and if you had told me, I would have been very offended. This is only one of the four major forms of inflation but a popular form among therapists, the one we naturally go to. It is the same with professors, priests, and other clergy. We naturally get into the magus inflation (see Moore 1996).

Then I became aware of John Perry's work, *The Self in Psychotic Process* (1953), *Roots of Renewal in Myth and Madness* (1976), and his book on the myth of the royal father, *The Lord of the Four Quarters* (1966). I thought I was just going to study the magician, but John Perry's work led me into studying the role of royal archetypes in transformation. Later I realized that sometimes the king does not just sit on the throne but goes off like Julius Caesar and leads an army. He becomes a warrior and commands warriors. The first time I taught from this format, I had three masculine archetypes: king, warrior, and magician. At that time I still could not see the *quaternio,* or fourfold nature, of the underlying structure. The "me-search" in my "re-search" was still leaving a major factor out, which I soon realized was the lover!

We have long known that integration of the "missing fourth" is a difficult psychological challenge. Most men in our culture, and possibly in many other cultures around the world, typically keep the lover part of them in the shadow, and they let women carry it for them. The typical agreement in a lot of old-fashioned marriages was that no matter what important things the man might carry, it was the woman who carried responsibility for the love dimension of the relationship. I had overlooked the poet aspect of my psyche that I had split off away from myself many years before. Before going to graduate school, I had been a rock musician, but then I split that part of myself off. Now I realized that I had to buy a Fender Telecaster again!

Thus I came to realize that Jung was right about the quadrated psyche, that the four major configurations did, in fact, exist, though he had not understood the contents of the quadrants. At that time I had not studied the ancient Egyptian concept of the self, so I didn't know that the ancient Egyptians thought the self had an eightfold nature and that one of the eight was your physical body. I also did not realize that sexuality and embodiment, and both the positive and negative qualities of the lover, usually come out in bodily forms. It is kind of a shock when you realize that people 3,500 years ago had some of these things figured out better than we do today. At the same time, it served as a helpful confirmation to find that some people in the ancient world also understood the eightfold structure of the archetypal Self, what Jung called the *double quaternio*. All these configurations exist within Jung's *coniunctio*, the inner sacred marriage of king and queen, and they are held in balance in the deep psyche, all symmetrically balanced in the deep archetypal Self of every individual.

Now let us look at the qualities of each of these configurations, the various qualities and kinds of space, and how inflation and grandiosity manifest themselves in the various quadrants.[3]

THE KING AND QUEEN AT THE CENTER OF THE COSMOS

First, there is the cosmos, the world, in the space that emerges between the king and queen. For the best treatment of traditional concepts of cosmos, see Eliade's book *The Myth of the Eternal Return* (1954). The ancients were always trying to find a cosmos as opposed to chaos. Chaos is all around, on all sides of the cosmos, and always impinging upon it (see diagram 5 in the appendix). So the king and queen on their thrones provide the archetypal center of the psyche, the *axis mundi,* that enables the world to be ordered against the forces of chaos (see Moore and Gillette 1991).

This is true in the individual psyche as well as in myth. If you carry a lot of anxiety, it probably means that you are not adequately connected to the king-queen aspect of your psyche. A narcissistic personality disorder identifies with the center, so if you look at them superficially, they will often not seem very anxious. They tend to think that they are the center.

The main problem with a narcissistic personality disorder, technically speaking in terms of the syndrome, is sensitivity to criticism. If you are a narcissist and people criticize you, you may experience great anxiety and fragmentation. When they are not criticizing you, and especially if they are constantly mirroring you, you may feel pretty calm with little fragmentation anxiety. You do not have to vibrate a lot as long as people are mirroring you, but people dominated by the king-queen configuration are usually very sensitive to criticism. Your anxiety level will stay fairly low only as long as you can arrange for everyone to adore you, because that serves as a camouflage and no one can detect how easily you become anxious and subject to fits of rage.

That is why so many of these narcissists rise to positions of leadership. They get a lot of adulation, and as long as they get uncritical adulation, they can look very calm and self-assured. They are calm because they are getting adored, but when criticism comes, their world begins to disintegrate. When the truth comes out, then everything begins to fragment.

THE WARRIOR

What diagnostic category might the warrior be centered in? There are a number of possibilities. The warrior is not sitting down there on the throne. What are warriors doing? They are fighting, yes, but warriors do other things in addition to fighting. For every fight that you get into as a warrior, you do a lot of other things. [4]

Audience: Strategize?

Moore: Strategize, right.

Audience: Questing?

Moore: Yes, you are always on a quest, but it is not like the mystical quest of the magician trying to find answers. If you are a warrior, you have your *mission*. You are not searching for your orders, because you already have your orders. Everything you do relates to your mission and your orders. What kind of personality do you recognize there?

Audience: Paranoid?

Moore: Well, it could be paranoid. The paranoid syndrome indicates a person who is being flooded with archetypal warrior energy. Warriors provide vigilance against the enemy, so a paranoid person who feels the enemy everywhere is shooting up warrior energy. The paranoid person is a grandiose, inflated form of the warrior.

But what else is there that is more of a garden-variety version? It probably applies to a number of us here today.

Audience: Obsessive compulsive?

Moore: The obsessive-compulsive neurotic is probably too ritualistic and too interesting.

No, I am thinking more of a compulsive personality disorder like that of the workaholic. Workaholics usually do not have any interesting obsessive symptoms; they just work all the time. Inflated compulsive people do not think they are God's gift to the world. That is more the style of the narcissist. What do they do? They just *act* as if they think they are God's gift to the world. They work all the time, because if they stopped working, the world might stop. Do you see the warrior inflation in that?

By contrast, if you are possessed by the king or the queen, you have nothing to do but sit there on your throne. You sit and you look at me. The Hindu traditions call this *darshan*. You look at me, and I look at you. I come into the ashram here and sit cross-legged on the floor. You sit on your dais over there so you can look at me, and I can look at you. The Hindu religious literature talks a lot about this experience. When I look at you, I can just feel the energy flowing. I feel myself being bathed in the love flowing from the guru. It's like getting an audience with the pope at St. Peter's. Archetypally, it's like going before the king and queen who offer me the eyes of blessing. The person in royal space doesn't have to work. You aren't running around all over the country giving lectures. You just sit there relaxed and cross-legged on your throne, offering me an opportunity to receive your royal gaze with all its constitutive blessings.

The workaholic warrior, by contrast, rides his charger off to do battle with the forces of death. That is my own natural mode. Many people who are compulsive in the warrior mode may not have great self-esteem, because it all depends on working all the time. If you do not work, you feel that everything will go to hell. You do not have much sense of peace. You feel a lot of hot, anxious energy. The warrior is a doer, not a be-er. You have heard the distinction between being and doing. People give workshops now on the theme, "Be here now." Well, that is exactly what a lot of people like me need to do. We need to learn to just sit and be (see Moore and Gillette 1992).

Audience: The warrior is the one who wants to save the world, right?

Moore: It is always the warrior, the one out there on the charger. Remember the Greenpeace environmental action group with a policy of nonviolent direct action based on scientific research? They didn't put the name *Rainbow Magus* on their ship protesting nuclear tests in the South Pacific in 1985. Nor did they call it the *Rainbow King,* or the *Rainbow Lover.* They called it the *Rainbow Warrior.* If you're going to take a little speedboat out to challenge a Japanese whaling vessel, much less the whole French Navy, it takes a *Rainbow Warrior.*

THE MAGICIAN

What about the magician? The magician doesn't sit on a throne like a king and give out blessings, and he doesn't accept mission impossible like a warrior and charge out to do battle with the forces of chaos. The magician tends to be more introverted in pursuit of *gnosis,* knowledge and wisdom. The magician is the arche-type of understanding and hermeneutics, the theory of interpreta-tion. This covers psychoanalysts, scholars, and interpreters of all kinds.

Do you realize that just to read all the books written in the aca-demic world in one year alone on the subject of hermeneutics would consume thousands of hours? If you tried to read all the technical books by Ricoeur, about Ricoeur, about the people who follow Ricoeur, whether Ricoeur is right about this, or whether so-and-so is right about Ricoeur, and then the relationship between Ricoeur and Gadamer, and the relationship between Derrida and Ricoeur, it would take you an awesome amount of time. But that is what academics do. They sit around and get ready for their annual meetings and worry about who is going to read what paper about what theory of hermeneutics.

Academics live in this world, and it is a wonderful world. I've spent much of my life in that kind of magician space. I love the search for detailed knowledge and understanding. That is where I started off early in my life and career. It is a beautiful and won-derful pursuit.

The creative people in archetypal psychology are excellent at this kind of pursuit of knowledge, the most prominent being James Hillman. Archetypal psychologists learn how to deconstruct everyone else's argument, because an inflated magus always has esoteric knowledge that is more incisive than yours. They always know better than you. Their hermeneutics are always more sophis-ticated than yours. They can always show that your methods of analysis are too literalistic or too simplistic, and they can go on for-ever with this. If a world problem comes up, an inflated magus will form a new study commission. When the world finally gets pol-luted to death, you will find an enormous number of scholars all tied up with study commissions studying toxic waste.

The magician is like a sophisticated technician who understands technical knowledge about how things work. If you are
inflated in the magician and not balanced by the other archetypes,
you would be like Sigmund Freud, who said he was more interested in developing a scientific psychology than in healing individual
people. Think about that now. "I want to know how things work,
and whether you get well is not as important to me as using the
data to design a scientific psychology." This kind of inflation
would tend to make you schizoid, unattached, and untouched
emotionally. You might not care very much about specific people,
but you sure would know a hell of a lot. You would understand it
if your analysands self-destructed. You would be wonderful at psychological postmortems. You wouldn't walk across the room to
help someone, but you would be able to write the most wonderful
case study for the institute after they had been carried out (see
Moore and Gillette 1993b).

THE LOVER

Where the magician is more introverted, the lover is more extro-
verted. With enough inner structure, the lover is usually sensitive
to others. For the inflated lover, if it moves, you adore it, and you
compulsively seek union with it.

If you are inflated with the king or queen (connected to them
in an immature way), you want others to bless and care for you. If
you are inflated with the warrior, if it moves you want to fight with
it and make war on it, because a warrior always has to have an
enemy. If you are inflated with the magus, if it moves you want to
understand it and interpret it. You don't necessarily want to do
anything about it. You just want to understand it and penetrate its
secrets.

If you are inflated with the lover, if it moves you want to lick it or put it in your mouth some other way. Babies manifest this. That is the body talking. That is embodiment. That is Freud's "polymorphous perversity," but there is nothing particularly perverse about it. It is just the lover manifesting. It is the sacramental human.

For the lover part of the psyche, everything gleams with beauty and luminosity. It is the sensation function. That is why so many intuitive personality types have the sensation function in the shadow. They act out in the realm of love and sexuality because it is so numinous for them. This part of the divine Self is in their shadow. They don't assume they know all about it, so when it appears, it truly seems to them like a manifestation of the sacred.

That is why the inflated lover can get into so much trouble, acting out and into addictions. An analyst from Montreal explained for one of our workshops how addictions were related to disorders of love. She was absolutely right about that. Addictions are disorders of the lover quadrant, because it is all very sacramental. You cannot get enough of whatever it is – food, alcohol, cocaine, sex, or you name it.

If you are a poet, or some other form of artist, this is what burns you out so often. You get burned out on this intense energy. This is why so many artistic people and poetic people self-destruct through self-medication, because the intensity of their perceptions is so powerful.

People plugged into the lover cannot pay much attention to the content of what is going on around them unless they can see an aesthetic beauty in it. They probably would notice how beautiful you are and look at each person in turn, and just go on looking at you. After this lecture today, a person who is in touch with the lover archetype might say something like, "Did you see the woman with that incredible necklace?" I would say, "What?!" but they would know what everyone was wearing, what their eyes were like, whether they were trim or tall. The lover in them appreciates each person's particularity.

It is amazing to be with someone like that, because they are like the Frenchmen on the curb watching the women walk by. A woman can go by who might not seem attractive to an American male, but a French male might say, "Wow. Look at those ankles over there!" Or he might say, "Look at the eyes of that woman!" People joke about that a lot, but in thinking about these things culturally, I think the French are much more comfortable with the archetypal lover than, say, people in German or English culture. English culture is more uncomfortable with the archetypal lover. That might have been what fueled a lot of the antagonism between the English and the French, the conflict between different arche- typal configurations. The English think that the French are so decadent, and the French think the English are so much more ascetic. You can go to England and have an ascetic spiritual expe- rience just eating a meal.

Audience: What about the difference between the different lovers in Hamlet? How would they fit into your outline?

Moore: They would be varieties of the lover configuration. Each archetype has many possible differentiations to the extent that the ego masters its potential. You can have higher forms and expressions of it, or regressive forms and expressions. An inflated person is possessed by its deepest and most powerful forms. For example, a really promiscuous person may have been terribly wounded in the lover part of their personality and now gets com- pensated by its grandiose energies. If you tried as a little child to love your parents, and they rebuffed you and hurt you, then your capacity for mature human love will be thwarted, and you might act this out sexually. Think about the Jungian theory of compen- sation here. Promiscuity often occurs in a person who experienced tremendous pain in the lover quadrant of their personality.

We have to understand both the archetypal loving couple and the polymorphous perverse lover, which is the archetypal lover. Krishna, the divinely incarnate teacher in the ancient Hindu poem *Bhagavad Gita*, makes love to everyone indiscriminately. That is the archetypal lover. Christ, the divinely incarnate teacher in the New Testament, also loves everyone indiscriminately. You may be the most ordinary lump of coal in the world, but Christ will look at you and see a diamond.

For the lover, if it moves, they just adore it. However, if you try to embody the archetypal lover in the real world, it doesn't work. It may work for a while. The movie *Looking for Mr. Goodbar* (1977) shows Diane Keaton as a borderline woman who is promiscuous because she was so hurt in her family that she acts out the Aphrodite pattern at night after work. Suffering and wounded in human love, such persons seek compensation, but compensation does not cure you without some sort of containment and interpretation.

Audience: Linda Leonard (1986) writes about the woman "on the way to the wedding," on the way to the sacred marriage, and she often talks about the sacred marriage of the *animus* and *anima*. Is that the same thing?

Moore: Yes. It is important to realize that the archetypal lovers are the king and queen of the other world, and they deal with each other lovingly.

If you want to understand the dynamics of the Oedipal problem, it is when the human male becomes the consort of the divine woman projected onto a human woman. Think about that now. The Oedipal problem for a woman is when a human woman becomes the consort of a divine male, projected either onto the father or onto other men. In this way you can understand Freud's classical teaching of Oedipal conflict archetypally.

When we are not clear that we are not going to be the consort of the king or queen, we have severe problems in our human relationships with men and women. If you are a woman and you project too much of the archetypal king onto your father, you will never turn away from him to an imperfect human man. If you are a man and you project too much of the archetypal queen onto your mother, then you will never be able to turn from her and form a committed love relationship with an imperfect human woman. You may have all sorts of human relationships, but you will not commit to them, because your commitment is to an archetypal personage that is being carried in projection by your parent (see Moore and Gillette 1993a).

SUMMARY

My purpose in this chapter was to show how a neo-Jungian approach using archetypal structures based on mythological resources can take analysis beyond the Kohutian understanding of the grandiose exhibitionistic self-organization. What the Kohutians do not know, and cannot know because they lack the theory for it, is that grandiose self-organization manifests differently in different people according to the archetypal configuration invoked in their family experience. Each individual's personal experience invokes or constellates particular archetypal patterns in the psyche and sets up the ways they will become inflated and grandiose when life experiences bring them to that point of regression.

The cornerstone of Jungian theory is the assumption that the human psyche is structured in a way parallel to Noam Chomsky's theory of linguistics. Jungians believe the human psyche contains deep structures. Contrary to what the ego-psychologist type of Freudians think, the unconscious is not just a chaotic cauldron of energy that has to be totally dominated by the ego. The archetypal unconscious, the *objective psyche,* is structured in a very clear way.

This project of mapping the inner geography of the archetypal unconscious seeks to improve our understanding of the central processes of human personality. The eightfold structure is part of my work on that mapping. It is similar to what Jean Bolen is doing but is not as dependent on particular culture-bound gods and goddesses as her work is. It is more of a role theory and draws upon a larger database of cultural and scientific sources.

Notes

1. This chapter is an edited account of the late afternoon session on Saturday, July 15, 1989, of a weekend workshop and discussion led by Robert Moore at the C. G. Jung Institute of Chicago in Evanston, Illinois. The original program was entitled "Jungian Psychology and Human Spirituality: Liberation from Tribalism in Religious Life."

2. For some of the revolutionary research unavailable to Jung that supports my decoding of these structures, see Robert Moore's taped lectures on *Georges Dumézil and "The New Comparative Mythology."*

3. See Robert Moore and Douglas Gillette, *King Warrior Magician Lover: Rediscovering the Archetypes of the Mature Masculine Personality* (1990). This introductory volume was followed with four other books, each describing in great detail how one of the four archetypes manifests itself in a man's personality.

4. See the taped lectures by Robert Moore, *The Collective Unconscious and the Shape of Psychopathology* and *Archetype, Compulsion, and Healing.*

CHAPTER 7

The Combat Myth and the Archetypal Enemy

ARL JUNG WAS CONVINCED THAT EVIL IS REAL AND A
powerful malignant force in human life. Any adequate
human spirituality must deal with the reality of radical evil, not just the personal shadow. We start with cross-cultural
expressions of the myth of the combat with evil. The psychology
of evil is not grounded in only one spiritual tradition, but in a
comparative mythology of evil that we now have access to for the
first time in history. Jungians specifically look for continuities
between these cross-cultural mythologies and the issues of human
illness and health.[1]

As shown in the previous chapter, my decoding of the structures of the archetypal Self delineates four inner couples presiding
over different psychic inner spaces: the king and queen, the warriors, the magicians, and the lovers. Mythologists throughout history have placed evil in the combat zone with the warriors who are
always fighting the enemy, archetypally speaking. Neil Forsythe is
not a Jungian, but he might as well have been, because his book,
The Old Enemy: Satan and the Combat Myth (1987), provided light
years of progress toward understanding the universality of the
combat myth. He has a chart that shows this cross-cultural layout
of the combat myth and maps the field of archetypal warfare, what

I have called the "plain of struggle" (Moore and Gillette 1992; Moore 1996). Sam Keen's book, *Faces of the Enemy* (1986), describes how humans always dehumanize and demonize people they perceive as the enemy.

My argument is that the combat myth is archetypal. It is in everyone's hard wiring. It is in the second pair of the four couples. It is inside all of us, and we must face it. When you are in the warrior mode, something will come up demonized, consciously or unconsciously. When you do not understand how the archetypal psyche relates to the ego, you will project the image of the archetypal enemy onto a human "other." It might be onto Reagan, or Bush, or the "Evil Empire," or the Jews, or the Muslims. In any case, you are acting out an archetypal shadow projection. Once you demonize someone, you load that person with demonic numinous energy. There is an interesting parallel phenomenon. Since you are hardwired for this archetypal enemy, when you identify with it you are colonized by it. Not the personal shadow that we are all supposed to integrate, but the archetypal enemy. You begin incarnating it in the world.

Can you think of anyone in the world today who might be identifying with the archetypal enemy shadow, with the very archetypal evil?

Response: Hitler?

Moore: Yes, of course Hitler thought he was a kind of messianic savior of his people. He modeled the S.S. troops after the Jesuits. That is clear from historical research. I am not knocking Jesuits, because I have an inner Jesuit myself. I am not a Roman Catholic, but I have this inner Jesuit that is always harassing me. A historian wrote a historical and biographical work calling Hitler the "psychopathic God" and documenting his rituals, how he had his own cathedral, and so on (Waite 1977). His identification with a messianic king was an aspect of his inflation, and in connection with the many other negative aspects of his grandiosity, it had demonic results. Grandiosity experienced unconsciously forms a "Lucifer complex" that becomes incarnate in our homes and communities as well as in world affairs. We become the actual enemies of cosmos or creative ordering.

Satanic groups actually consciously identify with the Lord of the Underworld. An interviewer recently asked a group of teenagers in a large city, "Why are you worshipping Satan?" They replied, "The end of the world is near, the final battle is very close, and we want to be on the winning side." So they worked on developing all the lore they could find about Satan.

If you study Jeffrey Burton Russell's books on the history of the mythology of Satan, and then study the psychology of narcissistic difficulties, you will see why so many people are attracted to Satan. People who have a problem befriending their grandiose energies in a conscious healthy way tend to admire Satan and identify with Satan. A lot of the old myths present Satan wanting to be seen as beautiful. That is exactly what *we* want.

Recent psychoanalytic research has helped us to understand this longing with more empathy. There is a healthy part of us that wants to be seen as beautiful and wants to be celebrated. Many traditions have given all the "glory" to God, which is fine for God, of course, but what if you also want to be seen as beautiful? What if you actually need and deserve a little of that glory? This is what Matthew Fox (1991) addresses with his "Creation Spirituality," that the creation has glory too. If you study sacral kingship and sacral queenship, you will find that the true king or the true queen always shares the glory. In fact, they are the source of glorification. They bless you. That is glorification. That is what makes you shine as a human. It makes you shine in your essential, beautiful, wonderful humanness. That is what Matthew Fox is trying to get at, and he is right about that. Religions have unwittingly fueled the attractiveness of evil by teaching that becoming more spiritual requires a depreciation and diminution of the human, and particularly the feminine. This widespread mistake has fueled both sexism and our current environmental holocaust. The great philosopher and theologian Paul Tillich counters this prevalent interfaith Manichaeism by asserting that the divine glory is present in every manifestation of being in a sacramental way.

If we set things up so that wanting to shine is demonic, then most people will want to be demonic. But Kohut made a great step forward in making it clear that grandiose energies were not necessarily demonic or bad. Your craziness is not because you have grandiose energies, but because you have not learned how to incarnate them in a conscious and healthy way that helps you become a radiant personality with healthy self-esteem. We have a lot of work to do in this area (see Lee et al. 1991).

Audience: You mentioned projecting onto the other the very thing that you hate in yourself, but isn't that just a phenomenon of psychology in general, that you become what you hate? In other words, isn't this why CIA agents use KGB methods to do their job. Or why we support democracies until they go socialist, as in Chile or Guatemala, and then suddenly we're not for democracy any more? Or we won't allow the burning of the flag and thus abrogate the very thing the flag stands for. In other words, it is becoming what you hate.

Moore: That is right. I recently saw a sign that said, "Your hate becomes you." You see this a lot now in Israel. One of these days we will have face what is going on in Israel. It is not anti-Semitic to criticize the Israeli army for using excessive force on Palestinians. We need to deal with that. We usually look the other way and do not deal with it very much, but it's the same type of thing. The entire conflict in the Middle East is being fueled by warrior inflation on both sides which is issuing in malignant tribalism.

This is unfortunately very human in an archetypal sense. Humans act out this archetypal inflation all the time, but it is not a conscious and morally serious expression. I am amazed at those people that say that Jung's thought does not deal with moral issues, because his whole psychology emphasizes the radical moral challenge of consciousness, and the challenge of withdrawing these archetypal projections. We must wake up and withdraw these things. Without awakening, we will never become more truly human and humane in our dealings with each other, other species, or the environment.

FACING THE GREAT DRAGON

We have to recognize that this inner reality becomes a terrible monster if it is not faced consciously with good will and intentions. It is archetypal, not human. It is not out there, but in here. It is often imaged as a giant, monster, or dragon. In many myths, you have to slay this monster. There is some monster you need to slay. In patriarchy it is usually imaged as a female monster. It is interesting that men would rather slay a female monster than a male monster. It is always easier to deal with the other gender's problems and put all of your shadow projections on the other gender. That is what the Oedipal concept is about. If you read Freudian Oedipal theory and get underneath it, you find this tendency for the boy to want to marry the goddess. This is the Attis myth. Down with the god. Take the god's place. In other words, there is a hidden god claim on the part of the boy. The girl wants to marry the god and displace the goddess. This is the hidden goddess claim on the part of the girl. Unresolved, these grandiose claims always lead to havoc.

We never quite get around to the actual slaying, except maybe in "Jack and the Beanstalk," but you intuit the need to "slay" your same-sex giant or dragon, because it represents this grandiose presence within. The only thing that can be slain, however, is an ego-organization that has merged unconsciously with the great dragon. The great dragon cannot be killed. It must be related to in a conscious way (see Edinger 1999). No matter how old you are, *you are not an adult until you have slain that unconscious identification with the grandiose presence within.* That is what human initiation is all about. Initiation is death. There must be a ritual slaying of this particular monster.

We love to tell everyone else to slay their monsters. Whatever my race is, I love to urge you to slay your race's monsters. Whatever my religion is, I love to tell you to slay your religion's monsters, but I don't necessarily want to slay mine. Whatever my gender is, I want the other gender to slay its monsters, even though I resist facing the monsters in mine. That is how it works.

Audience: I keep thinking of that awful news story where a bunch of boys attacked that young woman in Central Park. Isn't that the same sort of thing? Because they went after her, but all they said was they were "wilding." That was their excuse.

Moore: Yes, there are little boy kings, little unconscious gods, what I call "monster boys." *Unfortunately, unconscious grandiosity is an "equal opportunity employer."* It afflicts minorities and the poor as well as the privileged and the wealthy. If you understand this, then you can understand why we see such widespread and increasing anxiety and antisocial behaviors at all levels and all social locations in contemporary culture.

Unconscious gods have no limits in their fantasies. This is the satanic manifestation of the God image. The satanic impulse always has no limits. It is the mark of a Lucifer complex when you have no limits on your behavior or your claims. That is widespread, not just in men, but particularly in men. It is the runaway inflated warrior, the rape-and-pillage warrior, the Darth Vader warrior, because there is no true and good king to whom this kind of warrior is willing to submit and give service. This requires study of the history of the sacral king and the values in sacral kingship. The king's whole being was to create justice, protect the poor, and protect the weak. The sacral king had incredible radical morality and justice built into his responsibilities (Moore and Gillette 1991). Knights serving the sacral king were responsible for upholding those values and making war on anyone who was unjust, that is, anyone trying to bring chaos into the world.

The boy king, however, or the boy warrior, will use the enormous AK-47 firepower they have and turn it against their own community and against civilization. That is the difference between the shadow king or shadow warrior, and the true king or true warrior. Chaos and cosmos are always at war with each other in myth. The true warrior fights for cosmos, and shadow warriors want chaos. Any time two people come into conflict, we constellate the human tendency to clash and split. It is always the other person who is the partisan of chaos, while I am the pure one fighting for the right order of the cosmos. So we pair off and act this thing out, each carrying the shadow projections of the other. This is the tragic history of our species on earth.

In human affairs, if you study history, it has been a holocaust. That is not just one holocaust. If you study the history of childhood, that is a mega-holocaust. The history of women is a mega-holocaust. The more history you know, the less of a romantic, naïve, New Age, humanistic psychologist you will be. Those people like Professor Don Browning (1987) at the University of Chicago who equate Jung with Pollyanna humanistic psychologists are mistaken (see also Sanford 1987). The reason Jung got into trouble with Victor White was because he believed that the *privatio boni* doctrine did not adequately address the reality and power of radical evil (see Lammers 1994). Jung believed that radical evil was real, aggressive, and opportunistic. It is a psychic malignancy issuing in possession states where the unconscious human ego gets invaded and colonized by archetypal energies that it does not believe really exist or interprets in a fundamentalist, tribal religious framework.

We must distinguish between the Lucifer complex and the personal shadow. You can, as a human being, appropriately integrate your personal shadow. If what you call your shadow is only that part of you that wants to shine, then you need to integrate that psychological potential and become more radiant. The ego unconsciously identifying with the Lucifer complex, however, presents a far different situation. Jung talked about "spirit complexes" that you cannot integrate and must not try to integrate. If you try in a simplistic way to integrate yourself with the Christ complex, you will become psychotic.[2] If you identify with the satanic complex and begin to incarnate it, you will become a sociopath. The patterns of sociopathic behavior are very similar, because they are not personal but archetypal in their manifestation.

What are some other examples of the old enemies? Yahweh and who else? Baal. Zoroastrianism has Ahura Mazda, creator of earth, sky, and humans, and his enemy Ahriman, the destructive spirit.

What about the Hindu epic *Ramayana*? Does anyone know Indonesian and Hindu mythology? I recently traveled in Indonesia, and it is fascinating. They do not have very much television, but when they do, it is the *Ramayana* being acted out. When you go to the villages on Saturday night, and all the teenagers come out, they have their playhouse acting out the *Ramayana*. The *Ramayana* presents this great epic struggle, kind of like Beowulf, between the great Lord and incarnation of God whose name is Rama, the true Lord, and his enemy the demon Ravana. He is usually portrayed as having this incredible bright red mask. I have a great Ravana mask, and once you look through that you feel the power of the archetypal shadow.[3]

There are many other examples, Christ and Satan, for example. Any others?

Audience: Dionysus?

Moore: Dionysus is not usually considered an incarnation of radical evil.

Audience: Mars?

Moore: Mars is the god of war, but you do not get much of a clear split there. The more primitive mythologies are one thing, but the Greeks had many different stages in which they got their mythology cleaned up. You need to go back to some very old myths. You see this dual presence of good and evil more clearly the more archaic the mythic materials.

For example, people sometimes say to me, "What about Buddhism? There is no evil in Buddhism." They did not study Buddhist mythology but only Buddhist philosophy. The philosophers do not get into this too much, because it is too messy, but in Buddhist mythology, the Buddha clearly has to fight the lord of the demons. Very few have studied the relationship of Buddha with sacral kingship. There is an interesting story about Buddha, the true king, and Mara, the king of the demons. Sitting under the Bodhi tree, Buddha is almost ready for his enlightenment when Mara attacks with all the hosts of evil. Just as they are about to overwhelm the Buddha, he reaches down and touches the earth, and suddenly the demons are gone. Isn't that interesting in light of what we have been talking about?[4]

Audience: I was wondering what you make of the pairs. I just finished reading *The Chalice and the Blade* by Riane Eisler. I think she was saying that Baal would represent the goddess and the feminine, and Yahweh the nomadic conqueror would see that as being evil, even though it really was not.

Moore: Yes, that is right. I'm not saying these are really evil, but that the human mind tends to split and polarize. What I would disagree with here is that I think Eisler's view represents a feminine inflation: "If we could just return to the goddess, everything would be fine, because there are no arrogant goddesses. Only the gods are arrogant." That is just female grandiosity. All humans and all genders tend to inflate. They all have to struggle with their own temptation to try to be the center. So I don't agree with Eisler's book very much. It is just an inversion of the patriarchal problem.

Audience: Even though she prefers partnership to domination?

Moore: Yes, because Eisler demonizes the masculine in that book. Of all people, I am not one who will stand for demonizing the masculine. The masculine is not demonic. Men get inflated and act out demonically just as women do. I agree that partnership is a key idea, but I don't think Eisler's book is likely to facilitate much partnership.

Audience: In a world of nonduality, like some Buddhist and Oriental philosophies or theology, can you rise "beyond good and evil," like Nietzsche?

Moore: Yes, but Nietzsche is not a good example, because he rose up "beyond good and evil" into a psychotic inflation. When someone says they have risen up "beyond good and evil," it usually indicates an unconscious grandiosity. A magus who had achieved that state would not speak about it except in an esoteric inner community.

This is also true of many forms of New Age mysticism. They are incredibly inflated. They have no way to deal with their own shadow, so you get this enormous acting out, like the "great" Buddhist leader who recently contracted AIDS and carelessly infected many of his *chelas*. Not that they are any worse at it than Christians, Jews, or Muslims. They just have not solved the problem. Sitting around and meditating does not automatically enable you to face your grandiose shadow.

Audience: You indicate that by having a relationship with a Supreme Being, one should theoretically have less grandiosity and humanize, but you also imply that you need to have human relationship to bring you back down to earth.

Moore: I believe you need both. Grandiose energies are so present and so powerful in everyone's life that you need both resources. One is a connection with a positive transpersonal or archetypal center, and the other is participation in human relationships. They both remind you of the limitations of your ego, that you are a creature.

Jung was right about this. Without authentic and grounded relationships, you can easily get a little bit crazy, because you have no one to challenge your inflation. Human relationships in and of themselves are obviously not enough, however, because most people in relationships still have enormous struggles with their grandiosity. You need to form a conscious internal connection with what the Jungians call the archetypal Self as a center beyond the ego.[5] This helps the ego begin to get down off its throne.

We need more specific study of this. People are too vague about it. People are too vague about prayer, too vague about how to relativize the ego, too vague about how to establish and maintain the ego-Self axis. What are these things anyway? Can you tell me what they are? Are they just ideas? Or are they something real?

Audience: Is it possible for people to find individual ways to challenge their own inflation? Is it always the consequence of a relational situation?

Moore: I think it is possible for you to challenge it, and also important and necessary for you to challenge it. Let me give you an example out of my own life. I tend to get inflated in the warrior mode. Workaholism has always been my difficulty. I know that and I struggle with it. I use all sorts of things to help me deal with it, including more therapy and analysis than I care to remember. How much money I have paid trying to come down off that high chair! But it also helps to have a spouse who warns me before I take on one more workshop, one who asks me, "Don't you think you need to get some rest?"

To summarize, there is a great dragon of grandiosity within us, and unconsciousness of that fact creates a very real enemy within. It is a real human war and a real Armageddon, not against other humans but against being swallowed by the great dragon of unconscious grandiosity. Our war is against the pathological infantile grandiosity that seeks to destroy the human species.

Pogo said, "We have met the enemy, and he is us," but psychoanalysis makes it possible for us to refine that. I would like to sit down and talk with Pogo about this. I would like to say, "Pogo, I don't think our true human selves are the enemy. Our grounded and human creaturely egos are not the enemy. The enemy is that unconscious grandiosity within us that constantly tries to persuade us to forget our limits and forget that we need help, to forget that we need others, or as the Native Americans are able to say, to forget that we are all related and all of one family."

The bad news is that every single person has this dragon within, but there is even worse news than that, in fact, news far worse than the Freudians want you to believe. If my fundamental metapsychology were Kohutian rather than Jungian, I might get into the fantasy of being healed of my grandiosity. You might hear me say that I could be healed if only I had the right analyst, or if only I had a long enough time, or perhaps if I could be analyzed by Heinz Kohut himself. I might have a fantasy of one of those analyses that the self psychologists write about where grandiosity is supposedly so transformed, transmuted, internalized, and built up into such a true human self, that for all practical purposes it is essentially gone. Of course, they do not really claim that all the grandiosity is gone. They would never make that statement, but they will say, "You have to relate to the grandiosity, and you have to transmute and internalize it," sort of a domestication image. It is as if you had a wild bull, and you finally got him down to size so you could get him into the stable and go in and curry him, and so forth, images about getting him under control. Think of the Minotaur, the monster in Greek mythology. Getting the Minotaur into the barn would be a warm and fuzzy domestication image.

Self psychology is fuzzy on this. They do not come out on this clearly because they still are not sure about it. What is this now? Do we get rid of our grandiosity or not? Do we transmute and internalize our grandiosity into the human ego, into the human self, the healthy human self? Is that what we do? In that respect, if you have enough analysis, can you reach a point where you will never again have any more problems with pathological grandiosity? They have a fantasy that such elimination of grandiosity is possible. They may not admit it or talk about it, but they do have that fantasy.

A Jungian should never have that fantasy. A Jungian should know that there will always be a great Self inside that will never get completely transmuted and internalized. It is always in there, and here is the bad news, it will always press to take over. This is what explains why, after you work with someone for a while, they will say to you that they still have this problem. But what is it that they have? It is sheer fantasy to think that you can ever transform your grandiose energies so they will never seduce you again, that you can ever prevent your grandiosity from being seductive.

Sometimes people think if they just prayed enough, or went to enough masses, then their grandiosity would stop being seductive. Or if they became a cardinal, or a bishop, or a mother superior, it would not be seductive anymore. The truth, of course, is just the opposite, because the more successful you get, the more seductive grandiosity gets. The more traumas and tragedies you have in your life, the more grandiosity will attack you. It can tell you how impressive it is that you are still alive, or it can chide you into depression by suggesting you might as well go ahead and commit suicide. Many suicidal thoughts come from a grandiose perfectionism.

So Jung's point of view on this is much more vigilant than a Freudian perspective. You never get to the point where you are not vulnerable to the archetypal numinosity of the archetypal Self. Jung made this clear. He said, "Look, the Self is dangerous." A lot of Jungians do not understand this. They think the archetypal Self is always friendly, trying to help. Where they get that I do not know, but they do not get it from Jung. The archetypal Self, if you are not awake, will eat you alive. Jung made it clear that you have to take a moral stand in the ego against the pressure of the archetypal Self. You must engage it and decide which of its promptings you are going to include in your ego, and which you are not. We do not talk about this enough.

The spiritual traditions of discernment are enormously important, because you always have to listen to those voices you hear in your head and decide which ones are voices of demonic inflation trying to kill you or get you to kill someone else, and which ones are voices of the center trying to establish a just order in your psyche and the world. They are not the same voice. The voice of the true king and the true queen in the psyche is always a blessing and loving voice, a voice that brings peace and power to the personality. Voices in your psyche that do *not* bring you peace, power, love, and joy come from demonic aspects of the archetypal psyche that hate you because you are not perfect, or because you are too perfect. Envy is directly related to all of this. Envy rolls right off of the grandiose Self.

Audience: Yesterday you were talking about projecting a god or goddess complex on people.

Moore: Men or women. You can project it on either or both.

Audience: The way I understand it is that you project some expectations on someone that they cannot control, and one of them was not having limits. What would be some other basic ones?

Moore: For example, when you fall in love with someone and do not have any understanding of these dynamics, it can become an overwhelming possession. I get people coming in and saying, "I just cannot live without this person. If they leave me, I will die." It is as if you just met Astarte, the Phoenician goddess of fertility, or Isis, the goddess of the Egyptians, and you are mesmerized as one of her servants, and suddenly your autonomy and your initiative are gone, and your sense of self-worth is gone. You see this constantly in both sexes. This is an overwhelming idealizing projection of externalized grandiose energy, or god-energy.

The elevation to the pedestal is a fascinating thing. I have spent much time in the last ten years studying sacral kingship and sacral queenship (see Perry 1966; Moore and Gillette 1991). When you put the king on the throne, you must totally control them. That is what the Kohutians speak of as a selfobject transference. That is to say, if I get into a selfobject transference with you, you must do exactly what I want you to do, and if you do something that I don't want, then I am enraged with you. The whole kingship thing, the dynamics between the king and the people, directly expresses that. Many kings were never allowed to come out of their huts. The people never saw the king at all. Even the king's royal red carpet had an unexpected purpose, to keep the king from ever touching the ground. Many of the sacred kings were also not allowed to see the sun. Why would that be? Why should the kings be kept out of the sun? Think about it. Exposure to sunlight could depotentiate the king. If the "Sun King" saw the actual sun, he might not feel like the Sun King anymore, because he would realize that he doesn't shine nearly as brightly as the real sun does. Once the self-esteem of the king drops, the crops won't grow, and the cows won't have their calves. Then what happens? They have to kill the king. If the king gets too depressed, you have to kill him. He must be replaced. Today we call this "traumatic de-idealization."

Understanding this makes a lot of sense out of political and organizational behavior around leadership. You get a little blood in the water around your executive, or around your king, and the sharks begin to gather. Once the leader shows himself to be vulnerable, unable to carry the numinosity, then the human psyche has an archetypal desire to kill him and get rid of him so we can find another one who doesn't have that flaw. If the king has a flaw, the kingdom can't flourish. That is the old wounded Fisher King myth, but there are also wounded Fisher Queens. When I do active imagination with groups on this, I sometimes find a person whose queen is healthy, but whose king is sick. Or I find a person whose king is healthy, but whose queen is ill. It is fascinating to look at that if you know the archetypal dynamics. A whole range of things happens based on these archetypal dynamics.

Audience: Joseph Campbell talks about the collapse of mythology in general, and you talk about the collapse of the sacred canopy. Where do we go from here on this? Campbell says we have to go out and find it individually because the collective is not doing it. So where do we find that?

Moore: Yes, we need to address that question. Campbell's contribution is to say, "You need to become students of world mythology to enrich your understanding of the fullness of masculinity and femininity, and the richness of all human experience. Mythology will give you a vocabulary, a language to talk about matters of the soul." Campbell is right about that. It is time for us to do this. We cannot allow ourselves to be lost in tribal myths anymore. We must open ourselves up to the entire symbolic treasure, the human symbolic trust.

Joseph Campbell, however, was not a psychologist, and he did not pretend to be one. Some people try to turn him into a guru, but he does not make a great guru. His advice to "follow your bliss" may sound good, and now everyone talks about "following your bliss," but they forget that Hitler was following his bliss. If he could have followed his bliss a little longer, I for one might not be here today, because I have enough Jewish blood in me that I could have been burned in the ovens. Following your bliss can be a recipe for enormous ego inflation and destruction. So Campbell did not have Jung's genius for understanding the moral and spiritual discipline required to create and regulate the ego-Self axis.

Campbell does give us the imperative to learn human mythic language. His contribution is one big move toward a new global human Pentecost. The image of Pentecost is a great healing metaphor that counterbalances the image of confusion in the Tower of Babel. You hear all these different languages, but then you start thinking, "Now I can listen to this Islamic mythology and make some sense out of it as a human being." This is new. With Campbell and Eliade, we have reached a new level in our growing capacity to be good stewards of the entire human symbolic trust.

Why is this so important? For one thing, we need to understand that the patriarchal symbolism permeating our culture results from being lost in a narrow band of the spectrum of the world's mythic imagination. The archetypal psyche of the *coniunctio*, the divine marriage of king and queen, is expressed in all the world's mythologies, but only partially in each one. When people think they can solve the world's problems with a different myth, they are only offering to make you one-sided in a new way. The issue is to realize that we need to create a container, a chalice or grail, that holds with reverence the entire human symbolic trust and enables us to cherish it all.

Audience: *Bliss* is like a Sanskrit word *satchitananda* which means "bliss" in a very sacred way, not in a profane way, but we tend to "follow our bliss" in a Western way. Also I wonder about Jung's comment that a Westerner cannot grasp an Easterner's thought and vice versa, so that having a world view of mythology might be wrong for us, because our internal wiring would be, maybe, circuit A for Westerners and Circuit B for Easterners.

Moore: Yes, that is software from culture, the cultural unconscious, but the archetypal psyche is not software; the collective unconscious is specieswide.

Audience: How do you know? How do you know that it is not differentiated?

Moore: First, because I am not a racist, and second, because of the burgeoning scientific evidence that humans across the world are essentially the same primate animal. That is not to say I have no radical differences within myself. I carry Russian Jew, Cajun French Catholic, and Scotch-Irish Protestant, so I have a lot of the cultural unconscious within me, and I am quite clear that it comes from very different streams. We need to study how ethnic and cultural differences impact the unconscious. There is no question that there is a cultural unconscious, but in a Jungian framework the cultural unconscious is not the same as the archetypal Self or the collective unconscious. The instinctual collective unconscious is specieswide.[6]

I am a neo-Jungian on this issue. No one has to agree with me on it, but I think it is much more hopeful to assume a general human unconscious that serves as a base for the cultural unconscious, the family unconscious, and the personal unconscious. It is layered like that. I am convinced that any hope for unification and cooperation of people around the world is grounded in an affirmation of a common deep psyche from which we can reach out to each other. That is the importance of Campbell, Eliade, Jung, and the other people who are urging us to look at world mythologies as the human symbolic trust.

We will never get psychic wholeness by adding up all the myths and then dividing them by a hundred. That is the old syncretism. An authentically Jungian point of view is different from that. Jungian psychology in these issues is not theosophy, or even an attempt to find a "mono-myth." Theosophy tries to study all the world's religions as if they were basically the same, and then tries to develop a theology that unites them all. That approach is not Jungian. The products of the imagination are diverse and different, and any particular product of the imagination—whether a myth, a dream, or a philosophy, a theology, a psychology, or anything else—will only be one expression of the deep archetypal Self of the *pleroma,* and it will be uniquely structured, and it will be partial, not complete so as to cover all expressions.[7]

So we need to find other ways to relate to the wholeness besides adding up myths and coming up with a new theosophy. That will not work. That is another reason why Jung argued that Westerners should not appropriate Eastern ideas too quickly, or that Easterners should not appropriate Western materials. I differ from Jung in emphasis here. I think we must ask people to study the mythologies of other cultures even if they do not want to convert to them. It is essential for people to study and learn from the symbolisms and mythologies of other faiths and cultures than their own. All these materials belong to the human symbolic trust, a part of the inheritance of every human child. The entire symbolic *pleroma,* therefore, is a very important part of the human birthright and must be stewarded appropriately by all of us. Jung's work offers us a way to address this task effectively.

NOTES

1. This chapter is an edited account of the early morning session on Sunday, July 16, 1989, of a weekend workshop and discussion led by Robert Moore at the C. G. Jung Institute in Chicago, Illinois. The original program was entitled "Jungian Psychology and Human Spirituality: Liberation from Tribalism in Religious Life."

2. Mystics and magi of different traditions understand how to incarnate these energies in ways that are creative and not demonic. I am working on a book, to be titled *Riding the Dragon*, which will address the creative embodiment of dragon energies.

3. The classic Sanskrit Hindu epic *Ramayana* appears in many English translations and novelized retellings.

4. See Falk (1987). Additional background can be found in Ling (1997) and Boyd (1975).

5. On the ego-Self axis, see Edinger (1972).

6. Jungian analyst Margaret Shanahan has done extensive research into how the cultural unconscious impacts on individual appropriation of archetypal potentials. On the instinctual, specieswide unconscious, see Stevens (1982, 1993).

7. See the philosophical theology of Paul Tillich for an unsurpassed understanding of the limitations of language and symbolism.

CHAPTER 8

How Modern Spiritual Narcissism Leads to Destructive Tribalism

THIS CHAPTER REVIEWS OUR PROGRESS THUS FAR AND then looks at how all the psychological issues relating to the combat myth and the archetypal enemy work together to emerge as the problem of pathological tribalism.[1]

The Tower of Babel image illustrated how human infantile grandiosity brings individuals and groups into deep struggles to maintain their cohesiveness, and this leads them to great difficulties relating to each another. Any serious study of narcissism and narcissistic pathology, whatever your school of thought, will show that the greater the unregulated grandiosity in the psyche, the more difficulty the individual has with both symptoms and relationships. All the major schools of psychoanalysis—classical Freudianism, Adlerian, Jungian, and contemporary Kohutian self psychology—recognize the reality of a powerful grandiosity in the psyche that is not the authentic human ego, even though the ego often unconsciously identifies with it. In fact, the worse the parenting you received, the more likely your consciousness is contaminated with grandiose fantasies, wishes, and behaviors.

Almost all psychopathology, except what comes from biochemical deficits or organic failures, results from individuals not having had an adequate nurturing environment to let them down empathically and slowly from their little high chairs. We come into the world on a grandiose divine pedestal. That is what the Jungian understanding of the divine child is all about. This is perfectly normal and natural, but the task of human maturation must be to help the individual get down off of that little divine high chair and into a human position.

I love to teach comparative psychotherapy, because all therapies are trying to help you do that same type of thing, to be more realistic, to be less totalistic in your claims, to do less exaggerating, to do fewer behaviors based on some sense of entitlement or special exemptions, and help the individual to face limitations. All therapies tend to address these issues in some form or another.

We are in a position today to understand this phenomenon better. We should provide public education on this, however, and not let this understanding be the exclusive possession of a professional guild. We need to realize that the human propensity to grandiosity is universal. This is not a simple moralism. When people acted out in grandiose ways, the spiritual traditions were hard on them moralistically. Acting out in a grandiose way merely shows the seriousness of the wound. It is a sign of either excessive pampering or inadequate nurture. Self psychologists would say it indicates a lack of attunement with parental figures, how much impatience was encountered that tragically split off the child's godlike consciousness into the unconscious rather than employing its numinous energies to feed life, to inspire and fuel the child, and provide the strength needed for work and play.

We need to understand the universality of this propensity to unregulated grandiosity. I never met anyone who did not have a struggle with it. I have met a lot of people who didn't think they did. Some people have the illusion that psychoanalysis successfully transformed all their primitive grandiosity. You can only sustain such a fantasy of idealizing transference if you don't have to get along with very many psychoanalysts! Once you do, no matter what the school of thought, you soon recognize that they still have plenty of primitive infantile grandiosity left. Otherwise, their feelings wouldn't get hurt so easily.

Audience: What do you think about the feminist theory that every woman should raise her consciousness and discover "the goddess within"?

Moore: Absolutely, I think that is true. Every woman, and every man, needs to discover "the goddess within," but it is also important for them not to mistake themselves for it, or project it onto another human being. This is where a lot of contemporary voices do not help us much. The men's movement and the women's movement need to help individuals connect to the *coniunctio,* the inner divine marriage of the king and queen, but not to identify with it. What we call "problems of gender identity" in loosely organized personalities often result from overidentification with the *coniunctio.* The deep Self contains the king and queen in all of their forms. If your personality is loosely organized and without an adequately functioning ego, you may have a lot of androgynous fantasies. I would rather say that the deep Self is a royal couple than that it is androgynous. The two are very different. When the human ego thinks it is the royal couple, you have a lot of grandiose acting out. We increasingly have many people in our culture and around the world who unconsciously identify with the divine couple.

Audience: What does that look like on a practical level?

Moore: It manifests in individuals who are extremely confused about their sexual identity and simultaneously assailed with impulse disorders. Some new magazines are trying to get people to be complete in themselves, a sort of Madison Avenue autism. Think about that. That is why we need to have some psychoanalytic sophistication, because a lot of popular advertising is aggressively selling pathological narcissism as a normative vision for human life.

Certain circles today argue for a human norm based on the old autonomy fantasies, that the mature human is autonomous, adequate within himself or herself. This is just a symptom of pathological narcissism. When you work with people in their problems with relationships, and their problems with their own instability, you will notice that those individuals who are struggling to be one in themselves have enormous problems with their symptomatology and acting out. They have tremendous difficulty dealing with other real persons. They prefer fantasy persons, what we call the *anima* and *animus* projections, the nonreal person that you are in love with.

Robert Johnson's little book, *We* (1985), laid out a lot of interesting material on this. The person who carries the goddess projection for a man, or the god projection for a woman, is a real, human person. You discover this as soon as you have problems in a relationship. The little boy king in us, and the little girl queen in us, do not like it when our partners do not worship us uncritically.

People deal with this all the time. When someone treats you like a human being and does not worship you, to the extent that you are overidentified consciously or unconsciously with a grandiose exhibitionistic self-organization, you will have a rage response and a "grandiose retreat" into isolation. The more sensitive and easily hurt we are to nonadoring responses, the more it signals a possession state by this grandiose organization. When you find yourself having rage responses and withdrawing into detached isolation, such as when you say, "I do not need them out there, because they treat me that way," that is the angry king or queen. I should say prince or princess, because it is not a mature king or queen. There is much literature available on this.

To understand the dynamics of human evil, whether in the personality or the human community, you must look at the underlying dynamics of pathological narcissism. Scott Peck is right about that, but he is wrong to make it the province of only a handful of evil people. Narcissistic pathology is more like sin, a condition common to all. Spiritually speaking, you don't ask, "Am I a sinner?" You ask, "*How* am I a sinner?" So psychologically speaking, you shouldn't ask, "Am I carrying any narcissistic pathology?" You should ask, "Where is my narcissistic pathology? How am I acting it out? Where is my continuing residual unconscious, unregulated grandiosity possessing me and destroying my relationships?"

That is why, contrary to the Kohutian tradition, I delineate the different configurations grandiosity can take. The Freudian school can't give you a map, because they don't even study the collective unconscious, so they can't see the various archetypal configurations that unregulated grandiosity can take. Yet mythologies throughout history in all parts of the world have given us precise maps of these various configurations and responded to them.

Unregulated grandiosity expresses itself in different ways depending on how you were programmed in your family. The family unconscious will shunt you in a certain direction, and you will express your grandiosity in one form, and your sister will express it in another one, and your brother will express it in another. It is all unregulated grandiosity. The holy one and the hell-raiser are equally grandiose. They just express it in different archetypal configurations. My decoding of the archetypal structures, as presented in chapter 6, represents my research contribution toward providing a more adequate understanding of this.[2]

The spiritual traditions certainly never understood it. That is why we have what Reinhold Niebuhr called "spiritual pride." We thought that a really humble person was not grandiose, that an ascetic lifestyle was the same thing as humility. Discoveries in twentieth-century psychoanalytic theory, however, clearly show this not to be the case. That is why I talk to spiritual directors about subtlety in discernment. We have had a quantum leap in resources for discernment in individual spiritual direction since the origins of the various schools of psychoanalytic theory.

These insights, however, are radically more important on the larger level of planetary culture for anyone trying to provide adequate spiritual leadership for humanity at this time. The increasing difficulty now is that everyone's grandiosity is bumping up against everyone else's grandiosity. As long as your tribe does not have to deal with anyone else, it can have as grandiose a self image as it wants to, as long as it has ways to rationalize that it is okay. If you live in a hermitage, and you consider yourself the greatest spiritual athlete of all time, and there is no one else around that has to put up with your personality, hence no one around to criticize you for anything, then you can get away with believing you are indeed the greatest spiritual athlete of all time, the most humble man in the entire world. Once some other guy moves into the hermitage, however, then you have to start dealing with that other guy, and now there are two little boy kings, and little princes do not get along very well.

Audience: This is a problem that I have with a lot of the religious philosophies. I am thinking of one theologian who went into the woods and communed with nature and came up with a lot of wonderful ideas. But I keep wondering, if a woman had been living there with him, they might have spent a lot more time arguing over what the hell they were going to do next.

Moore: I have always said that the greatest antidote to pathological narcissism is a relationship with a real person. That is why grandiose people have difficulty with real relationships. To the extent that you don't deal consciously with your grandiosity, you won't be able to stand real human beings. You will either try to dominate them or seek to be dominated by them.

Many mythologies have the gods and the goddesses constantly warring in a sort of mythology of family life. If you study world mythology, you will see the dysfunctional family of the gods, and then you will understand us humans better, because we are their children. When all our great marital therapists die and go to heaven, maybe the gods and goddesses can finally get some good marriage counseling! What if you got Zeus and Hera together, and you said, "We are having a lot of problems here among your children on earth, and we think it is probably because you two don't deal properly with your relationship." It is fun to think about family systems theory in terms of world mythology and the relationships between the gods and the goddesses. It is a fascinating and playful thing to do, but it is grounded in the serious issues we have been talking about, because primitive grandiosity does not want to acknowledge and respect any other center of divine power. You get this fantasy that there is only one throne, while the problem in any relationship is that there must always be two thrones. Otherwise it will be a sick relationship.

Audience: Doesn't the healthy impact of relationship on narcissism make a strong argument for a noncelibate clergy and also for marriage counseling for married people?

Moore: I recently attended a conference where a male priest and female priest were co-celebrating, and they were wearing rainbow stoles. In practicing "active imagination," I tried to image the great royal couple. I thought, "There is my *coniunctio*, right up there, leading this Mass." It was really lovely.

It might help the Holy Father to have an articulate, brilliant, passionate, sexual wife. It would help him ground his infantile grandiosity, and his spiritual director would have a lot less to worry about. The boy king in him would have some help in coming down. I am not arguing for or against celibacy, but I can imagine the benefits the pope would get from marriage. Remember how archetypal projections can inflate your grandiosity. Think if you were the pope. It would be a real spiritual problem to deal with your grandiosity because everyone constantly dumps their idealizing projections onto you. It would be a tremendous problem. If you think the priest has a problem, the bishop has a greater problem, the archbishop has an even worse one, and if you were trying to be the spiritual leader of all the millions of Roman Catholics in the world, think of carrying that archetypal burden. Think about going around the world and having 400,000 people gathered in front of you idealizing you while you do Mass. This man obviously has to be relatively healthy emotionally in many respects or he would become greatly disturbed.

So clergy have a huge emotional challenge. Just because you are ordained doesn't mean that your shadow disappears. I deal with clergy all the time who have massive problems managing their own grandiosity. They tend to act out a lot. In fact, the phenomena of clergy acting out sexually, or in substance abuse, workaholism, or any other compulsive behavior, relate directly to the problem of managing their inner grandiosity. Clergy burnout is nothing in the world but a manifestation of grandiosity and the inability to regulate it. We need to work with this a lot to get more conscious of the problem. If we are going to pretend to provide spiritual leadership to the planet, we have to provide some spiritual leadership at home first, in terms of getting up every day and having our own ritualizations to help us contain and channel our grandiose energies.

We need to set up our own personal and spiritual ritual practice so we understand what we are doing. Many people who teach about prayer do not realize what they are dealing with, because they do not understand the radical power of these grandiose dynamics in the psyche. Once you begin to understand what a great struggle against infantile grandiosity we all have, then you will understand how important prayer is, and liturgy, and active imagination, and consecrated objects. (See chapter 10 for more discussion.)

Audience: When you talked about male-female relationships, you seemed to imply that marriage was a great thing for wholeness. Doesn't marriage as an institution have just as many pitfalls as the institutional church? Isn't there always a potential sickness in the marital relationship?

Moore: There is such a thing as marital dysfunction, yes, but there is a struggle against narcissism in all relationships.

Audience: But can we really say that marriage supports wholeness? Marriage as an institution seems problematic to me. Isn't relationship the key factor?

Moore: Right, but I am not a sociologist, so you would have to talk to a sociologist about the sociology of these institutions. I am a psychoanalyst, and what interests me here is what marriage does psychologically. Murray Stein writes of marriage as a vessel, the creation of a crucible that can help both people deal with their problems. The fine book by Harville Hendrix, *Getting the Love You Want* (1988), also treats this particular issue, not institutionally but emotionally. What you need is a container that allows the real people to emerge and gives them enough support so that they do not immediately leave.

We need creative ritualization. We really blew it when we depreciated the importance of ritual in the Enlightenment. We need ritualized containment with human beings in relationships to help people manage unregulated grandiosity. You have studied the history of ritual and human communities. Ritual is a technology of dealing with this problem. We create ritual forms that help us be less destructive. The history of human ritualization is the history of people struggling to find ways to be less destructive. That does not sound pretty and romantic, but that is how we are.

No, marriage is certainly not perfect, but it can still help provide some containment for working with the psychodynamics of life. This is what Harville Hendrix tries to point out. The family is not a perfect vessel, but it can provide a lot of containment for helping people down off their high chairs.

HOW PERSONAL PSYCHODYNAMICS LEAD
TO MALIGNANT TRIBALISM

How then do these personal psychological issues relate to the problem of destructive tribalism?

The human psyche develops over time, and numinous tribalism was one stage that gradually developed in human consciousness. At one time in human history, outstanding leaders carried most of the group's grandiosity. The pharaohs of ancient Egypt functioned that way.

This evolution of kingship is fascinating. (Certain matriarchal cultures probably had a similar roles for queens, but we have fewer records of that.) The king was not at first merely a human being. The Egyptian pharaoh was not a human being but a god. Over time he gradually transformed into a sort of deputy or earthly aspect in service of the god. John Perry's useful book, *The Heart of History* (1987), discusses this, and I have been influenced by Perry in this area. Frankfort's book on *Kingship and the Gods* (1948) also traces this development.

These dynamics work gradually something like this. Humans have always known they must do something about the solar furnace within, because it is creative and wonderful, but also seductive, and when it comes up and burns you, all hell breaks loose. The book *Anthropology and Evil* (Parkin 1985) describes many tribal traditions associated with this idea. All these traditions, in spite of their different languages, found the same force lurking about inside that was creative, exciting, and wonderful, but could also go bad and create enormous problems for the community. There is substantial anthropological evidence for these traditional understandings.

Humans began to realize over time that they had erred in these kingship forms by putting all sacredness on the kings and then totally controlling them. With continuing progress in psychic differentiation, we gradually enlarged the arena of sacralization for carrying the idealizing projections. The container for grandiose energy gradually got larger and larger until the group itself, the tribe, became sacred, that is, became the vessel for idealizing projections and infantile grandiosity. We constantly project this numinosity on many different cultural and religious forms and social groups of all kinds. We use numinous tribalism, in other words, to displace our rampant grandiose energies.

Let me give you an example of how this numinous tribalism might express itself in American religious terms that we can all understand. Suppose you meet me for the first time, and you start talking with me. You see that I don't have an unrealistically inflated image of myself, that I certainly don't think I am God, for instance. In fact, I may seem very humble to you, and as we talk you think to yourself, "Surely this person has no problem with grandiosity. He is not lording it over me." Soon, however, you get to know me a bit more, and suddenly you discover, to use a Southern example, that I belong to what is known in some parts of the South as the Church of Christ.

Audience: I started out in the Church of Christ in Kentucky.

Moore: Then you know what I mean. Let's just say this example comes from the Church of Christ as it exists in Texas and certain parts of Arkansas. I don't want to generalize too far. Suppose you talk to me some more, and you learn that I belong to the

Church of Christ, but you think to yourself, "That's fine. There are a lot of different churches around."

You talk to me some more, however, and you discover that I believe that only members of my church can have a right relationship with God. When I find out that you are a Baptist, or a Methodist, or a Catholic, or a Jew, or whatever, all of a sudden our relationship changes, because you realize that I believe you are one of the goats, and I am one of the sheep!

An enormous psychic split has opened up between us. I may even have family members who are not part of my particular "elect" group. It is very difficult to believe that your family members are condemned to eternal damnation because they are not members of a particular church.

Audience: That actually was true in my family. We had members of my family that were not a part of our church, and there was a lot of pain.

Moore: Oh, enormous pain, because you love them, and you want so badly for them to be "saved." We form these selfobject relationships to groups, and, technically, they are not separate because we are the selfobject. When a particular group is a selfobject to me, then for me that group *is* me. It carries my idealization and my grandiose energy, and I will begin to fragment if it stops containing and carrying the numinosity, the god-complex, and is no longer divine for me in this special way. I can no longer maintain my human ego structure or self-structure after the group I identified with stops carrying the numinosity for me.

These groups play a crucial role in people's lives through the selfobject relationship, seeking to displace grandiosity onto a social form like a group or religious "tribe" in an unconscious attempt to regulate grandiose energies. Unfortunately, however, this kind of mechanism usually sanctions a depreciation or even demonization of other people that results in hatred and fuels the genocidal impulse.

This demonic process occurs in all kinds of social groups, not just with religious ones. Marxism, for example, functions the same way for a lot of people. I know some people who have to struggle to accept me in spite of the fact that I am not a Marxist like they are! They are in great conflict about me, because they cannot demonize me as easily as someone they don't know as well. They know that I am very committed to social justice, but they also know that I refuse to be as blind to the many Marxist atrocities as they are.

Race is another vessel for displacing grandiose energies. We all have this kind of selfobject relationship to our own race. Whites are not the only racists. As you move around the world and study the planetary cultures, you find that racism is extremely wide-spread. It is an equal opportunity disorder of the human psyche. The more you travel, the more that becomes clear to you. The reason for racism is very simple: the need for selfobject transferences to particular, discreet affiliations that enable us to displace our grandiosity, avoid personal fragmentation, and act out unconsciously in grandiose ways. Therefore, the less conscious capacity to regulate grandiose energies, the more racism.

This function of racism is portrayed in the recent movie *Betrayed* (1988) about a white supremacist paramilitary group. It shows the attraction of Nazism among American youth and poor, marginalized white people. They use their selfobject relationship to the white race to define their circle of affiliation so as to demonize other groups, whether they be Jews, blacks, Catholics, or whatever. People inside the circle carry numinosity, for they are the elect ones, the chosen people, the people of God. People outside the circle are the people of Satan. You can call this whole process "the psychodynamics of the elect." It is a big part of the Judeo-Christian-Islamic shadow, but all spiritual tribes are afflicted with it.

The concept of a specially chosen group of the elect is a strategy of the psyche to maintain its integrity and selfhood while trying to cope with its own grandiosity. That is my argument. Whether you agree with it or not, I just ask you to follow it. We constantly struggle to disown our grandiosity because we have an intuition that it can make us psychotic, that it is destructive, that too much of it will kill us, so we spread it around as much as possible on groups of other people. I will get you people to help me carry my load of grandiosity as long as I can keep the sense of grandiose entitlement.

For example, if you start thinking like a pop Jungian, you will share your personal grandiose numinosity with the group known as Jungians, and you suddenly realize that other groups have little to offer. You no longer have to study other theories, other traditions. You can even study Jung with people who were blessed in an apostolic succession coming in a direct line from Carl Jung himself. The Jungian community has a lot of this apostolic succession nonsense: "Who laid their hands on you?" We have a fantasy of passing on the magic baton from one generation to the next.

Thus a Jungian can demonize the Adlerians, the Freudians, and everyone else, and not have to study other theories or learn anything from them. You can always tell which Jungian analysts are doing this, because they usually know nothing about the other theories. They know nothing about recent Freudian materials, because they don't think they need to consider them, and Jungians already have the Holy Writ. Some even talk about the "Black Bible," because Jung's *Collected Works* are contained in twenty volumes bound in black. That is an extreme example, of course, but understandable in terms of the psychodynamics involved. The Freudians modeled this behavior, and the Adlerians are no better. Every human group does it.

In this phenomenon of splitting, people try to maintain their sense of significance, specialness, and goodness by excluding other people. It is a universal human tactic, but demonic and destructive. The next step in our evolution requires us to face and transform this pattern.

Audience: I'm trying to understand how this works. Are we fragmented by *not belonging* to an exclusive, special group where we feel like we are one of the chosen ones? Or are we fragmented when we *do belong* and think we are part of the chosen group?

Moore: Belonging to a special group is an unconscious tactic used to avoid fragmentation of the ego, but not everyone uses this tactic. People having an enormously difficult time managing their grandiose self-organization and its energies may handle it in different ways. That is an interesting part of studying this particular phenomenon. Some people seek to regulate it by drinking a lot, others by compulsive sexuality, so that we need a twelve-step program for sex addicts. Others handle it by going to Mass every day. All these self-soothing methods help in the struggle to regulate troublesome grandiosity.

Other people displace their grandiose energies by disowning them: "Oh no, I'm not proud, I'm humble! But the group I belong to is the most exclusive group in the world. We will go to heaven and leave everyone else behind. I am a humble person myself, but the great cosmic spaceship is coming soon, and it only has room for 144,000 people to get on board. We can't be sure about that. It may only have room for 144, or 14.4, or 1.4, just enough room for me and a small part of someone else!" No one wants to lose touch with their grandiose energies and become more depressed. We just don't want to face it consciously.

Audience: Would you still be just as fragmented while belonging to such an exclusive group?

Moore: No, because your ego is not fragmenting if the group serves effectively for you as a defense against your grandiosity. You are no longer being fragmented after you join a group that can truly contain your grandiosity for you. Belonging to a group perceived as an adequate container enables you to offload your personal grandiosity onto the group and say, "I personally am not so great; I am not God."

Your unconscious grandiosity still functions beneath your repression, but you regulate it through the psychological prosthesis of splitting it off onto the group. This psychological tactic enables you to function more or less normally and appear more psychologically developed than you really are. Without such a prosthesis you would have to face the dragon consciously and either continue consciously the processes of individuation or become psychotic.

A person in a group can say, "This group is a new cult, and everyone outside it is doomed, but me personally, I'm humble, and I'm just doing what God wants me to do." In the context of this social group, I am humble, and so are all my fellow members. Everyone in the group is humble. We can be humble precisely because we belong to a group that has the only tickets available for seats on the great cosmic spaceship that is just about to come.

A recent movie named *Cocoon* (1985) directed by Ron Howard told the fantasy story of a spaceship coming down to earth on business and giving some old folks a chance to go with them when they left. The folks at this particular rest home decide to get on it. That is a movie version of this archetypal fantasy.

Regulating grandiosity is a universal human need, because everyone has to deal with this same great dragon within. We are not stupid. We have an inner magician, an inner magus, our Merlin or Gandalf, whispering in our ear, saying, "Robert, if you get any more great, you're moving toward a severe psychosis, so you need to get a bigger vessel for your grandiosity. You better join a more prestigious group to help you out with this, one where you won't be so great individually. Those people can help you carry your personal dragon. You can get together with them and line up and carry this great dragon together. It's much easier than consciously facing your own dragon alone."

The newly humble people still have to contend with the great dragon, but now it's a function of the overall group, not the conscious responsibility of any one member. By the way, sometimes the individual's little boy king and little girl queen get really angry about all this humility. Even though they are still allowed to exist, they no longer get enough conscious and direct adoration inside the humble person. That is why people who try to be humble unconsciously hate the fact of their humility at the same time. The little boy king and little girl queen within us really hate it when we stop acknowledging them consciously, and this fuels a lot of envy, hatred, and violence. This psychic process explains the politics of envy, why so many people with necrophilia out there would love to blow up the world. You have to understand how the little god within feels when it is not adored.

Audience: Is that directly related to the theory that you are talking about? The exclusivity, the exclusiveness of each different group?

Moore: Yes, but why do we do that? You see, if we didn't have the Soviet Union, Reagan's "Evil Empire," it would be harder for Americans to deal with their own personal grandiosity. We wouldn't have such a demonic enemy to be superior to.[3] We think the communists want to take over the world, but that peace-loving Americans don't want to take over the world or anything else. We don't want any of that world market! Note how easily our grandiose shadow traits become so invisible that we cannot confront our own arrogance.

That is why Gorbachev's reforms are creating such a psychological crisis for the West. He doesn't act like Satan is supposed to act. We unconsciously wish he would invade another country, or act like the Chinese, for instance. Chinese leaders are far more helpful, because they act just like we unconsciously want them to, which gives us a wonderful focus for our satanic projections. We can say, "Oh, it is really evil over there in China!" If they stopped being difficult, we couldn't project the evil shadow upon them quite so easily, and that would force us to start dealing with our own emotional problems and shadows. America would face a psychological crisis. That is how it works. When someone refuses to carry your projections, it creates a psychological crisis for you. Your displacement mechanisms no longer help you regulate your own grandiosity, so your ego must look for another way to avoid the truth.

What can you do about this kind of situation? Are we condemned to keep on acting out like this? Does it have to be this way? No, I don't believe that for a minute, but if I were Jimmy the Greek, and you asked me what the odds were that humans will keep this up until they self-destruct, I would have to say that the odds are pretty good.

Suppose, for example, that you had to make that bet. Suppose there was a spaceship that could take you somewhere else, like the star Sirius, and let you escape from this world. Would you take the odds that the human species will keep on going the way it has in the past and keep escalating violence until it destroys human civilization? Or would you gamble that people will suddenly start learning just before it is too late and take dramatic action toward awareness and responsible behavior? Personally, I must be a gambler. I think there is at least a chance that we as a species can beat the odds against us, but only if we all do our part in facing the dragon of grandiosity.

To win this gamble as a species, however, we have to start with a rigorous conscious look at the problem. A neo-Jungian framework can help us understand the psychodynamic origins of these problems. Contrary to what a lot of my liberation theologian friends seem to believe, no political ideology will solve these problems. We have to understand the plumbing.

Everyone is wired with this same dragon of grandiosity, this same solar furnace, this same god-complex, but these inner realities find different outer expressions. The energies can be contained through conscious ritual practices or mythic forms or get displaced into relationships and create division, demonic splitting, and projection. When the energies have nowhere to go but onto the ego, they make you psychotic. When they go into idealizing another person, they make you masochistic and dependent. You can even play the role of masochistic slave if you can find someone willing to play the role of sadistic god. Displacing the energies onto a limited group results in a malignant tribalism where tribal exclusivity is important because it helps avoid individual psychosis.

All these things have been going on for a long time, but our satanic, Faustian refusal to wake up and consciously face these great inner realities has more ominous implications today than ever before. We not only have weapons of mass destruction now, but the human population has grown so large that rapacious consumerism threatens to destroy the planet's ecology. Deforestation, like the destruction of the rain forests, proceeds at such a rapid rate, I think, because of the grandiose, rapacious appetites of people who have become secularized and modern in their cultural viewpoint. This is an important argument to understand. Culturally modern people who retreat into secular individualism have fewer places to contain their grandiosity, so they tend toward self-medication excesses like consumerism, the cults of beauty, celebrity, or addiction, or some other kind of addictive pseudo-spirituality. Prophetic voices from all the world's religions rightfully criticize these forms of malignant narcissism.

To stay with the ecological problem, our planet simply cannot sustain the current rate of archetypally fueled, compulsive consumption. There is massive denial on this subject by both spiritual leaders and political leaders. They think they have accomplished something significant when they get together with a group of world leaders and say, "We must do better at this!" Just the ecological issue by itself should be enough to make us realize that we have to address global grandiosity or face some very unpleasant consequences. That should be more than enough to make us face up to the dragon of grandiosity.

Another issue just as large, however, is the problem of proliferating weapons of mass destruction in an age of terrorism, which in my view is a ritual phenomenon. Our species is preparing unconsciously for a transformative ritual that will try to kill the dragon. We unconsciously intend to "nuke" our own grandiosity! The unconscious orchestrates this. Douglas Gillette and I have an unpublished manuscript entitled "The Last Rite" that brings together the apocalyptic myths of the world in this context. This drama of a great burning is in the human psyche.[4]

World leaders need to learn about these archetypal pressures toward either transforming or destroying our global grandiosity epidemic. In my view, we must either have a new spiritual revolution that *consciously* confronts global human grandiosity, or we will soon engage in a literal but *unconscious* sacrificial ritual that seeks to cure this human cancer by self-destruction. In other words, if humanity will not consciously face its problem of grandiosity and spiritual narcissism, then the unconscious alternative will try to cure the malignancy by nuclear cauterization. We must either face the global initiatory task consciously or be doomed to act it out unconsciously.

Audience: Would you say that God wanted us to push the nuclear button? Or does he give us a choice?

Moore: That is a theological question, but I personally believe the choice is ours. Unconscious grandiosity always carries a terrible price. The scriptures of virtually every religion clearly identify human grandiosity as a major problem. Even evolutionary psychology is beginning to recognize that religions evolved as a tactic to help humans regulate their grandiosity (see Wright 1994). We must accept the challenge of awareness and regulation of these dragon energies.

Audience: Do we not have the Garden of Eden with its tree of knowledge?

Moore: You can do a lot with that myth, and many other similar ones reflect the difficulty of handling the seduction of grandiosity. Men, of course, love to blame this seduction on women, and vice versa. Everyone wants to put the responsibility on someone else for succumbing to the temptation of unconscious infantile grandiosity, because this temptation is the hardest thing to deal with and sacrifice. In the Babylonian epic of creation, the local male god Marduk was the only one who could defeat Tiamat, the great female dragon of chaos who personified the primeval oceans. This was viewed as a great heroic feat, but it would have been more impressive to me if he had killed a male dragon, because men have more trouble facing the great male dragon. In real life, as in Beowulf, one must face both male and female dragons.

NOTES

1. This chapter is an edited account of part of the morning sessions on Sunday, July 16, 1989, of a weekend workshop and discussion led by Robert Moore at the C. G. Jung Institute in Chicago, Illinois. The overall program was entitled "Jungian Psychology and Human Spirituality: Liberation from Tribalism in Religious Life."

2. These matters are also discussed in my unpublished lectures, *The Collective Unconscious and the Shape of Psychopathology*, audiotape 597, and *Archetype, Compulsion, and Healing*, audiotape 655 (Evanston, Ill.: C. G. Jung Institute of Chicago).

3. We should all notice how much anxiety levels (even *in utero*) have increased since the "end" of the Cold War. This is no accident. It makes a great deal of sense if put in the framework being discussed here.

4. See Edward Edinger, *Archetype of the Apocalypse* (1999). I totally agree with Edinger's assertion that it is futile for humanity to try to repress the unconscious imperative toward individuation.

CHAPTER 9

The Psychological Sources of Religious Conflict

I T IS A PLEASURE FOR ME TO BE HERE AND TO WELCOME YOU. This symposium is a labor of love and cooperation of a number of institutions: the Chicago Theological Seminary, the Institute for World Spirituality, the Center for Jewish-Christian Studies of the Chicago Theological Seminary, the Organization for Universal Communal Harmony, and many other persons and contributors who have contributed their funds and their time and their devotion to the importance of this topic.[1]

Let me just tell you a little bit about my method here, what we hope will be "the method in our madness." I want to thank especially the people in psychology and psychoanalysis whose work I will be sharing with you in an ecumenical way. While I am a Jungian psychoanalyst, my first book was a Freudian book, and my first psychoanalytic diploma was an Adlerian diploma, so I am not here simply to represent my own work, but to try to speak to the changes, the discoveries, the knowledge in the psychological sciences that has developed since the first World Parliament of Religions in 1893. I want to bring some resources to you, as Paul Tillich would say, "to frame the human question," and we are going to proceed in this symposium on what he would call "the method of correlation." I will speak as a human scientist, as a psychoanalytic scientist, reporting to you on some findings on the human condition that have occurred since 1893.[2]

We will cover here some material that is difficult but extremely important for understanding the seriousness of what we face today in terms of jealousy, envy, and hatred, and what I call "malignant tribalism" among human ethnic groups and, in our context, among religions. We will first contextualize this as a specieswide problem. Then I will share with you some relevant insights from psychoanalytic traditions since 1893. Finally, I will frame some questions that persons from the great spiritual traditions in this symposium can respond to later.

Our first task is to face the shadow side of our species. Many forces today seek to deny the human tendency toward malignant tribalism and genocide. Some persons and groups around the world, for example, seek to minimize the horrors of the Nazi Holocaust or go so far as to deny that it ever happened, ever existed. Some have rewritten textbooks to deny the degree and severity of the evil perpetrated on fellow human beings through racism, sexism, and blatant genocide.

A recent book by Jared Diamond entitled *The Third Chimpanzee: The Evolution and Future of the Human Animal* (1992) traces the evolutionary background of genocide. It severely challenges the common denial that humans have engaged for a long time in genocidal behavior. We know more about familiar recent examples, and they perhaps frighten us more because of how we have put the highest technology into the service of genocide. We need, however, to understand that genocide has been a human tendency for at least thousands of years, and that specialists in primate studies can describe sociobiological roots of this kind of behavior.

This tendency to create a vision of the "other" that depreciates it and legitimates murder, and even genocide, is a widespread phenomenon, not just in our species but in other primate species as well. The idea of the "noble primates" that never hurt anything is a fantasy uninformed by the facts. One of my colleagues who has researched this more completely than I have tells me it is a good thing that we are more closely related to chimpanzees than to baboons, because if we were more closely related to the baboons, we would already have had the final nuclear holocaust. So we need to get serious about looking at the evidence about the tendencies that come with the species that we are.

What is this tendency that we have as a species? It is this. The problem we face is that we rationalize malignant tribalism and genocide. We put the forces of our intellect and all our other resources into rationalizing, helping ourselves accept these types of behaviors on the part of human beings. There are two fundamental ways this kind of behavior has been rationalized in the history of human genocide.

Our first rationalization of genocidal behaviors is based on self-defense, the classic picture. We feel ourselves in a dangerous position. There have been attacks upon us, and those attacks are utilized to dehumanize our attackers to the degree that we lose touch with any sense of their humanity, and therefore lose touch with any sense of limits on our responses or reactions. Diamond's book goes deeply into examples of that. The chief result of this tactic is to deny the humanity of the other people. It may even go so far as to ascribe nonhuman languages or nonhuman essences to them. So you can insert the name of the religion that you prefer to hate when you say, "the so-and-so swine," or "the so-and-so dogs," or "the so-and-so wolves," or "the so-and-so rats."

Diamond points out that this use of language actually works to facilitate the necessary psychological mechanism operating here, what psychology and psychoanalysis know as "splitting," the capacity for a trick of the mind that helps us forget that the problematic other person or group still belongs to our species. This is why it is so hopeful and encouraging to us at this conference to see conscious attention being given to the need to create a specieswide ethic or, to use Vice President Gore's language, to create a global ethic that recognizes a common human unity and respects other species as well.

We also tend to use religion as a resource to rationalize malignant tribalism and genocide. Every serious student can cite examples of how people of all different races and traditions have used religion to rationalize torture and murder. You can fill in your own knowledge at this point.

When we look for psychological and psychoanalytic resources to understand this situation, the person who understood these phenomena most deeply was Erik Erikson (1902–1994). He called this problem a human tendency to pseudo-speciate by which he meant falsely creating a new species category to account for the existence of those people you hate and no longer want to treat as human beings. This is the psychological dynamic. Because of failures in our own psychological development and maturation, or because of arrested development in what we might call our psycho-spiritual maturation, we tend to split the other off from ourselves and see them as nonhuman.

Now to achieve our goal of preparing to hear from spiritual leaders later in the symposium, we need to focus in on this issue of splitting. What is it? What causes this splitting? From Freud, the first great psychoanalytic genius, to the present, the testimony of the psychological sciences has been pretty constant on this, that the human psyche is extremely fragile. It is much more fragile than people tend to realize, and this applies both to human individuals and to human groups. Anytime the human family faces a nonempathic environment that is not supportive of its worth and sense of significance, it tends to start becoming disorganized in what Harry Stack Sullivan (1953) called the "self-system." It begins to come apart, to fragment, and that is the root of what we call splitting. There are many excellent psychoanalytic treatments of this topic.

In our context here, we need to realize that jealousy, envy, and hatred leading to violence are some of the most toxic by-products of this splitting, and thus toxic by-products of human environments that we ourselves have either created or allowed to develop. We have not faced honestly enough that we ourselves are responsible for those environments that are non-nurturing, nonempathic, and nonsupportive of the human soul and thus create this splitting and result in these by-products. This is a new psychological way of thinking about an old human problem. Psychoanalysis today uses a new technical term for this: "disintegration products." Think about that. Say it to yourself: "disintegration products." If you can get your thoughts around that, then you will understand a lot of what I mean. We all need to think seriously about what is it that we do, or avoid doing, that leads our brothers and sisters to become so fragile and so ready to fragment in their emotional life and therefore behave in ways characterized by jealousy, envy, and hate.

Let me just run through a few of these great pioneers and thinkers, and a few of their terms that you can study later on your own. As many of you know, I am a Jungian analyst, and I teach here in Chicago at the Jung Institute, but I will save Jung for last. Let me begin with Sigmund Freud (1865–1939). I am not a Freudian, but Freud knew a lot of important, true things, and one of the things that he knew and emphasized was the enormity of the difficulty of human beings learning how to overcome hate and how to love. That is the center of Freud's genius in every aspect of his work. He knew how difficult it was for all of us to learn how to love, to get beyond our narcissism, to learn how to love physically, to learn how to love interpersonally. He gave us deep insights into these tasks, into our ambivalence, and into how even our loves tend to get us into trouble. When we get to jealousy, we will see an example of that.

Freud's early colleague, Alfred Adler (1870–1937), the founder of Adlerian psychology, pointed out that our troubles result from a superiority complex that strives for power over other people. People who are psychologically immature engage in what Adler called the "depreciation tendency." Rather than organizing the world horizontally in terms of community, they organize the world vertically so they can step on others to become higher, better, and more acclaimed. Alfred Adler had a simple way to explain this. Behind every claim to superiority he found an underlying sense of inferiority. Every superiority complex has an inferiority complex holding it up. Conversely, every inferiority complex has a superiority complex beneath it.

What then, according to Adler, is psychological health? How can we get beyond jealousy, envy, and hate? We must first locate the source of our inferiority feelings. Why do we feel so inferior? What do we need in terms of encouragement so we can participate creatively in the human community? Adler said that the mark of emotional health was *gemeinschaft Gefühl*, that is, community feeling or social interest. We become healed psychologically to the extent that we reach out to other people and feel connected to them and cooperate with them, in spite of our differences. You can cooperate if you keep your mind on the task at hand rather than on your own superiority. The inability to cooperate comes from a pathological superiority complex. We can thank Adler for that idea in the context of the great task that we face here together.[3]

Another one of Freud's great successors, Melanie Klein (1882–1960), was a child psychologist who did some of the earliest significant work on jealousy, envy, and hate. Melanie Klein traced the roots of jealousy and envy back to very early experience. She emphasized how fearful the infant is even at an early age, and how much anxiety there is in a world where you cannot be sure you will be able to maintain your connection to something good, your mom. You cannot be sure whether your feelings toward your mother will be able to keep you connected to her or whether they will destroy her. So we all have a fear about being able to find the good, what Melanie Klein called "the good breast." By this she meant all the good in life, to connect with it and to maintain connection with it, and to deal with the feelings of rage when it is sometimes taken away (see Klein 1984, Vladescu 1997). These fears continue to haunt us as adults and often intrude when we are attempting to form meaningful and trusting relationships with others.

Let me call your attention to a New York psychoanalyst, Ann Belford Ulanov, whose book, *Cinderella and Her Sisters* (Ulanov and Ulanov 1983), is a revealing study of envy that I recommend in the context of our work here. Ulanov points out that envy appears when you feel disconnected from the good, when you feel that you have no good in you. It manifests when you feel you do not have a sustainable relationship with what is good in the human community or the human family. When I feel that I am not connected with the good, or not connected with the good as much as you are, then my reaction is one of hatred of you, and it can be an implacable hatred. Most of the implacable hatred in our world results from malignant envy. It comes from the feeling, "If I do not have the good, then you shall not have it either." If you will think about how much behavior in our planet has to do with trying to destroy that which others have, even their lives, then I think that you will understand how significant envy is in this context.

Another person who helped me understand this was Harry Stack Sullivan (1892–1949), an enormously influential and important theorist for this context. Harry Stack Sullivan distinguished between envy and jealousy. He saw a fundamental difference between envy and jealousy in the interpersonal situations in which these processes occur. We cannot go deeply into this, but we can say in summary that envy usually occurs between two people, you and me. Jealousy never occurs within a dyadic situation but only between three or more people. It works something like this. I love you (the first person), and I also love and esteem you (the second person), and the two of you have a relationship with each other, and I fear that I am not worthy enough, or I am not significant enough, or I am not important enough, or I am not beautiful enough, or I am not wise enough, to hold your attention and your relatedness.

To take an example, suppose I am a Christian, and I see that you as a Muslim have begun to have a relationship with a Hindu in my community. As I see the two of you gaining in esteem and love for one another, then I become subject to feelings of jealousy. This is very important for us today. Here we are all gathered together at the World Parliament of Religions, and we may think, "Isn't it wonderful that we are all here together?" Yes, of course, it is wonderful, but there is also jealousy. I see the Sikhs relating to the Jains, and the Jains relating to the Hindus, and I wonder, "Will they be interested in me? Or will I lose out here, and they will only love each other, and not me?" We speak of "the human family," but my friends, we are the human family, and we have just as much envy and jealousy in our human family as we do in the typical family. That is the bad news I bring.

Harry Stack Sullivan says that jealousy, like envy, is based on a sense of inferiority, that it comes from lack of a sense of worth. Either I am not worth enough for you to love me, or you will love someone else more than you love me. This reality impacts everyone – productive people, successful people, beautiful people, or personable people. The great psychoanalysts of the last hundred years have taught us that the more you shine, the more you will be the target of jealousy and envy.

Do I mean that if I manifest more religious wisdom, it will create more hatred of me by other religious people? Absolutely.

We must face the fact that envy can lead us to hate others because of their spiritual attainments. We must remember that we have spiritual gold coming from all these great spiritual traditions. We must be aware that when we see someone with spiritual gold, there is something in us that gets envious and says, "I have nothing like that" or "My gold is not as deep as yours." This may never come to consciousness, but it is a human tendency, not a Jewish, Christian, Sikh, Hindu, or Muslim tendency. Envy is a specieswide tendency. When we see others with gold, to the extent that we have not flowered into our human maturity, we begin to hate it and feel that we are cut off from it. That is the fundamental difference between jealousy and envy. Jealousy fears being left out in the cold. Envy leads to an empty despair that seeks to destroy the other.

One of the Chicago institutions I am grateful for is the local Freudian Psychoanalytic Institute, which was the home of one of the great revolutionary geniuses in psychoanalysis, Heinz Kohut (1913–1981). I recommend that we all study his work and the work of his followers, known as psychoanalytic self psychologists (Kohut 1971, 1985). One good reference is Ronald Lee's book, *Psychotherapy after Kohut* (1991). Another is by a social worker here at the University of Chicago, Miriam Elson, called *Self Psychology and Clinical Social Work* (1988).

Heinz Kohut was the analyst who helped us understand more sensitively than ever before the human need for recognition and affirmation. Now granted, Adler understood this need, of course, and Harry Stack Sullivan, and Jung, and all the other great psychoanalysts understood it, but they never understood it with the clarity of Heinz Kohut.

We like to talk about people's narcissism. "Oh, so-and-so is more narcissistic than so-and-so." We talk about "malignant narcissism," or the "narcissistic personality disorder," and the tendency of people to want attention. Today, for example, we have all these spiritual leaders at the World Parliament of Religions who parade in their religious dress and want attention from everyone else. We say, "Isn't that awful? Isn't that just the ego showing? Isn't that malignant narcissism?"

Heinz Kohut's colleague and his collaborator Ernest Wolf (1988) once said something like this, "Religious people will forgive anyone practically anything except their legitimate need to be seen and recognized." Kohut tried to help us understand the universally human need to be seen and recognized as significant, worthwhile, and meaningful. His work has helped us understand and have more empathy with this universal and fundamental human need.

What does this mean for us? My friends, I think we need to face how difficult it is for us to become empathic with other spiritual traditions and accept their legitimate needs for recognition and affirmation, their needs for being seen and given significant respect. Why? Kohut said that when we were children, we had not yet developed what he called "the cohesive self," or what we would call a self-system that is integrated and stable. What we needed from others he called "mirroring." We need to be seen. We need to be recognized and affirmed. You and I in our spiritual traditions would say we need to be blessed. We long for an experience of blessing.[4]

Kohut said that if we did not get enough of this affirmation and recognition as children, our self-systems would be unstable, like a building without any reinforced steel in it. Our infantile grandiosity is not adequately regulated and leaves us hypersensitive. So when the disappointments of life, which always come, hit us, if we have not had adequate nurture and blessing from the significant others in our life, then the house of our self will fall down. Lack of mature self-esteem throws us back into compensatory infantile grandiosity with its characteristic tendency to rage, hate, envy, and violence. Our capacity to function appropriately disappears as our personality fragments. Once the house of our self-system has fallen down, the result is jealousy, envy, and hate, and a willingness to join in malignant tribalism, violence, and genocide. We must understand that rage is always an indication of the failure of a human self. Rage is never the proper solution to any problem. Mature anger seeks cooperative solutions. Rage simply seeks the destruction of the other.

Kohut put two words together to help us understand how important this was, the word *self* and the word *object*. He said we have "selfobject relationships" with each other. We have selfobject relationships with other religions. What does this mean? It means that if you, my selfobject, my Jewish selfobject, my Christian self-object, my Sikh selfobject, my Muslim selfobject, my Hindu self-object, and so on—if when I look into your eyes I do not see any recognition or blessing, then I tend to go back immediately to the traumas and the curses of my childhood. Not to the blessings, but to the curses, and I begin to fragment and feel rageful toward you and your religion or tribe.

From the traditional indigenous cultures you have all heard of the evil eye. When we fail to get proper recognition, we tend to go back to the experiences of the evil eye that we all had in childhood, and we feel the anxiety and the fear, the insecurity, and the danger that we experienced then.

To sum up Kohut, what is the result of selfobject failures and disappointments? My whole self-system as a human being, my capacity to maintain a nonpsychotic state, is threatened. I fear that I am becoming disorganized. My anxiety begins to peak, and my paranoia begins to heighten. I begin to act in ways that see you as my enemy, and I begin to treat you in ways that will certainly tempt you to become my enemy. In Jungian analysis we call this phenomenon "shadow projection." It is a major factor fueling the contagion of hatred and violence.

So from Kohut's psychoanalytic point of view, jealousy, envy, hate, and violence result as by-products of experiencing an inadequate selfobject milieu or developmental environment of significant others, whether in America, India, the Middle East, or Eastern Europe. Such an inadequate developmental environment interferes with our need to be seen, recognized, and respected, our need for support in the task of developing the golden flower of a mature human being. Jealousy, envy, and hate result from an environment that fails to recognize that there can be no mature psychological or spiritual selfhood without the community, the great community that gardens selfhood and seeks to be a gardener of human selfhood and maturation for everyone on earth.

What does that mean? Rage always results from injuries to the maturation of the self sustained in a non-nurturant environment. Human experiences of neglect and resulting chaos always breed rage, and rage always results in more chaos. That is why human mythologies from all over our world link chaos with hatred and consider it fundamental to the nature of human evil.

We know that all human tribal traditions and all the great traditions of religious and spiritual communities have seen these realities of good and evil, and they have all spoken about them within the context of their own communities. In 1893, however, psychological science had not yet developed enough for us to see how clearly this is not just a Christian problem, or a Muslim problem, or a Buddhist problem. Now we can see that the things these traditions have long noted are not just local problems but constitute a universal human problem, a specieswide problem that requires us to work together at this World Parliament of Religions with every resource from each other that we can find.

We need to raise these questions to each religious and spiritual tradition: What does your tradition have to teach us all about the development of empathy for others, for the stranger, for those without adequate nurture and blessing? We must remember that without empathy you get rage, and then violence. What does your tradition have to teach us about discerning and confronting human arrogance and grandiosity? What does your tradition have to teach us all about mutual respect, and how we can facilitate it? What does your tradition have to teach us about the facilitation of a nurturing, affirming, supportive community? Using the word from our own spiritual traditions, what does your tradition have to teach us about facilitating a community that *blesses*? What is it that your faith can teach us about an optimum human, selfobject milieu for the human community? These are the kinds of questions that bring us together at this symposium.

We can look at the *New York Times* today and see how poorly we are doing at helping human beings feel the kind of self-esteem they would need in order to put away their weapons and start rebuilding a habitat for humanity and our friends from other species all over the world.

Is there hope? I want to get back to the tradition of Carl Jung (1875–1961) before I close. The great Jungian psychoanalyst in England that I admire, Anthony Stevens, recently wrote a book called *The Two Million-Year-Old Self* (1993), in which he wrote about the increasing scientific evidence that we have a blueprint within us to love and cooperate with each other, part of our birthright that comes with being a human being. It does not automatically build anything by itself, however, but requires a nurturing community to evoke that potential and unfold it into the golden flower of the human personality.

Carl Jung long ago affirmed the collective unconscious that unites all of us before we are Christian, before we are Jewish, before we are Sikh or Hindu or Muslim. It is deep in our DNA, with more than two million years of wisdom built into it that we should to try to nurture and evoke.

Jung also thought the human DNA had within it the capacity to allow us to experience what he called the "transcendent function." When we run into a situation of opposition, where there seem to be conflicts and opposites, the "transcendent function" within us wants to aid us in overcoming the obstacles and bridging the conflicts. That is biological. There is something in us that wants to make a bridge and create solutions and relationships. Even when we do not have the kind of relationships with each other that we need in order to nurture solutions and enact them effectively, the "transcendent function" is still in there seeking expression. There is something in us as humans that longs for this bridging and the peace and reconciliation it brings.

So, is there hope? I believe this human "transcendent function" is functioning in Chicago here today, and that the human "transcendent function" in you is working, and we soon will hear what the great traditions have to say about the divine ground and presence in this human possibility.

Today we can see the innate potential of this two-million-year-old self as a priceless resource. If we do our work together in this symposium and in the rest of this Parliament of World Religions, we can take encouragement from each other, and learn how to deal with the jealousy that we have because "all of you are loving each other and I may be left out." We might move beyond envy to a celebration of our mutual radiance. Then this conference may mark not the beginning of the end for our species, but the end of the beginning.

Notes

1. This paper introduced a Symposium on "Jealousy, Envy, and Hatred Among the World's Religions" at the Parliament of the World's Religions held August 28 to September 4, 1993, in Chicago, Illinois. The program was planned and coordinated by the Institute for World Spirituality. The introductory remarks included a special thank you to President Ken Smith of the Chicago Theological Seminary and to Dean William Myers, who made possible the original funding for this event. Also special words of appreciation to Dr. Andre LaCocque, my colleague at the Chicago Theological Seminary and the director of the Center for Jewish-Christian Studies, and to Ron Kidd, whose work has been important in putting not only the World Parliament centennial together, but this particular symposium.

2. To these ends I want to thank psychologist Margaret Shanahan, my wife, for teaching me much of the material that I will share with you here, the C. G. Jung Institute of Chicago and its many staff and supporters, the Alfred Adler Institute of Chicago, and the Chicago Psychoanalytic Institute.

3. On Adler, see *The Individual Psychology of Alfred Adler* (1989), *Superiority and Social Interest* (1979), and *Understanding Human Nature* (1927).

4. On the mythological and psychological foundations of the human need for and capacity to give blessing, see Moore and Gillette (1991).

CHAPTER 10

Resources for Facing the Dragon

Everything now depends on man: immense power of destruction is given into his hand, and the question is whether he can resist the will to use it, and can temper his will with the spirit of love and wisdom. He will hardly be capable of doing so on his own unaided resources. He needs the help of an "advocate" in heaven.... The only thing that really matters now is whether man can climb up to a higher moral level, to a higher plane of consciousness, in order to be equal to the superhuman powers which the fallen angels have played into his hands.

—Carl Jung

WHAT RESOURCES DO WE HAVE FOR CONSCIOUSLY confronting and regulating our grandiose energies? This chapter examines some of the psychological and spiritual resources available to us to deal with these issues in a more effective way than we may have realized was possible.[1]

GLOBAL DREAMS

Many Jungians today look at individual dreams to become more conscious of the collective situation. They engage in a comparative study of the dreams of people around the planet. They find, for example, that people all over the world are dreaming about an approaching world crisis. Some Jungian analysts have studied the

dreams of children around the world and found they were dreaming about a great crisis and coming conflagration. That offers us a
powerful image of how the unconscious is responding to our situation in the world today.

In a difficult world situation, people in therapy may have very
scary dreams that are not personal dreams at all, but dreams that
seek consciousness for the larger collective world. We should consciously open ourselves up to this prophetic dimension of dreaming and let it inform our discernment of personal leadership in
areas of social concern. It is not grandiose to raise the question of
how we can do our part. It is a move toward realistic grounding of
our spiritual life. This kind of listening should include taking seriously the growing consensus among the spiritual leaders of indigenous peoples that a critical time of decision has come for our
species and our planet. I think they are right that we are living in
a great *kairos* time that requires a great psychological and spiritual
awakening.

ACTIVE IMAGINATION

Reclaiming active imagination seems even more important to me
than studying dreams. Active imagination, in my view, is an
extremely powerful form of prayer. Christians have used the power
of active imagination in many forms for a long time, particularly
in the Roman Catholic tradition. These practices included the
spiritual exercises of Ignatius and a lot of other forms of dialogue
with Christ, with Mary, and with the various saints. Before we got
so smart that we decided we didn't need to have mythic dialogues,
you could dialogue with a saint any time you needed to. Every
spiritual tradition drew upon these resources in the past, but in the
modern secular world, we became so "smart and sophisticated"

that we threw out such imaginal dialogues. That was a terrible loss. We need to rediscover the practice of active imagination with our spiritual saints – our inner magi.

You can also do active imagination with the great king and queen within. From my point of view, if you want to talk about it theologically, that is a powerful form of prayer. A book came out about ten years ago that got a lot of attention for a while, *The Origin of Consciousness in the Breakdown of the Bicameral Mind* (1978), an interesting book by Julian Jaynes. His theory was that there once was a time in history when people talked directly to God, and people actually heard God's voice. Then we came to a period of evolution in which human beings lost the capacity to talk to God directly. He thinks the change resulted from a change in brain structure.

In my view, however, this change did not result from evolution of brain structure but rather from human beings forgetting how to do active imagination. Does this mean that human beings can still have conversations with the spiritual presence? As a Jungian I would have to say, "yes, in active imagination." If you have direct contact with the king and queen within you, you will not engage in idealizing transferences, that is, you will not nearly as easily displace your center or your sovereignty onto an outside person. More importantly, you will not identify your own ego with "the great royal one." When you are dealing directly with the sacred king and queen inside, you will not project them onto some human being in the outer world or merge with them unconsciously.

When you do active imagination, you go on a visualization journey inward. I recently led a group of people to the chambers of the royal couple within, and they had conversations. Some of them, however, did not find a king, some of them did not find a queen, and some of them did not find either one. Some found the royal chambers, but they could not find either a king or a queen.

Depth psychologists can have a field day thinking about what might keep a person from finding a king or queen when they go into their inner castle. Some go into their inner royal room and discover themselves. "Here I am!" Others discover their mom or dad. If you find your mom or dad on one of the thrones, or if you find yourself there as the queen, or yourself as king, then it can help you understand what is carrying your grandiose energies in an unhealthy way.

Some people think that such active imagination techniques are phony, that it is just "the ego making it up." Those people have never tried it, because once you do some active imagination, you are amazed at what these inner figures can tell you that rings a bell of truth but you somehow didn't know. There is no way to prove that to you except to invite you to try it. If you don't know what you need to do about your grandiosity, just ask for an audience with your inner royal couple. They will be much more confrontive about it than I am.

You may have a hard time finding them. They may be out there in the spaceship *Enterprise* saving some planets somewhere in another galaxy. I don't know where they are when they aren't home, but you can ask them. My experience after doing this with people for hundreds of hours now over the years is that if you keep going back, you eventually make contact.

Sometimes you may run into Ivan the Terrible or someone like that, but once you understand how this works, you can follow Jung's advice and say, "I know who you are. I know why I had such a bad experience, because I have been thinking that you were my father." You must speak up to them, forming conscious contact and more adequate, respectful boundaries with them.

In active imagination, you need to make sure you can get out and run if you have to. You might need to escape. You might need Ariadne's thread. You may have heard of the hero Theseus who took Ariadne's thread down into the labyrinth. For my analysands, I do not recommend a thread. At the very least I recommend a 100-pound test deep-sea fishing line, maybe a nylon rope, so you can find your way back out of there fast in case it gets ugly. Start with Barbara Hannah's book, *Encounters with the Soul* (1981), or Robert Johnson's *Inner Work* (1986). Also see his little book, *We* (1985), which shows the implications of this for relationships, and his book on *Ecstasy* (1989) is a good meditation on how to keep from going crazy when you become wonderful (see also Jung 1996, Ulanov and Ulanov 2000).

I hope some day to do some writing on active imagination and spirituality, but a lot of people are writing about this. Don't let them scare you to death about it. It is not as dangerous as a lot of people want to think. Leaders with a real magus inflation may imply to the group, "Be very careful how you do this. Only we initiates know how to do it right." You should be careful, that is true, but don't let yourself be intimidated by people telling you to be afraid of it, because then you won't do anything with it. It is a lot more dangerous to *avoid* doing it!

Active imagination is no doubt one of the most important tools we have for confronting and regulating our grandiose energies. Jesus reportedly said "the kingdom of God is within you" (Luke 17:21 AV). I think there is a lot of merit to that comment, but it is equally important for us to realize that "the king and the queen are within you." It is one thing to have a kingdom within you, and you go in there and don't find any kings or queens, but if there is a king and queen, a *rex* and *regina* within you, it is important to go in there regularly and talk to them about what is happening to you and what you need to be doing. My experience working with overly anxious people is that their anxiety level drops considerably when they do active imagination with their king and queen. It is a creative and useful way to relate to your dragon energies.

People should try this approach and see what they find out. I invite readers to write me a note and tell me the results. Tell me if you succeeded in forming an active imagination relationship with your inner king and queen and whether it helped your anxiety states. There is no guarantee that it will help everyone, but there is much to gain and little to lose in trying it.

EXERCISE PROGRAM

Another way to create a personal ritual to contain and channel grandiose energies is a regular exercise program three to five times a week. It is amazing how much craziness in a human personality can be controlled by the ritual of an exercise program. Some studies show you can manage a sizable depression problem successfully with regular exercise. For many it works as well or better than antidepressant medication. It is certainly much better for your health if you can gradually get off the pills and get "addicted" to your exercise program instead. Of course, even the best exercise plan in the world cannot substitute for conscious, psychological analysis with a competently trained analyst or therapist, but it can always be part of the package.

Think of the regular exercise as part of your ritual practice, a conscious ritualization in your ongoing spiritual discipline. Let it become a liturgy for you, marking sacred space and time. It will get to where you feel uncomfortable if you do not do your regular run or workout on Monday, Wednesday, and Friday, or Tuesday, Thursday, and Saturday. It is striking how easy it is to tell if you missed part of your healing ritualization, because your grandiosity will kick up on you. When you miss your exercise program, you become more compulsive in other ways. This is a rule that you can follow. Take it to the bank. You will act out more destructively to the extent that you do not tend to your physical discipline. This is part of the Zen, the Zen of exercise, an important resource for all of us.

RELIGIOUS COMMUNITY

Religious community can also help many people contain their grandiose energies, though this has become more problematic for many people today. Participation may help you avoid terminal fragmentation by allowing the group to carry your unregulated grandiose energies. The more primitive your grandiosity, the more the group you seek will believe in its exclusive legitimacy.

Audience: Are you saying that a person without such a problem of grandiosity no longer needs to belong to a group with such beliefs?

Moore: Well, everyone *does* have an ongoing problem with grandiosity. That is my key point. The question is, what do they do with it? Different people develop different strategies to contain and regulate their grandiosity. The more consciously confronted and regulated one's grandiosity is, the less one will need to have one's spiritual or ethnic tribe make foolish superiority claims.

You just have to ask yourself, How do I contain and regulate it? What do I do to keep from unconsciously identifying myself with the god or goddess? We all do something. We do a variety of things. If you are narcissistic, you unconsciously act it out, compulsively seeking adoration by other people. Group membership often helps and is a major resource in many cases. It is important not just to provide a vessel for the numinosity, but to have people who will remind you when you are getting a little crazy. This is why isolation is so dangerous when you are struggling with your grandiosity. When the negative manifestation of the dragon wants to destroy you, it tries to get you alone.

People who cannot connect with a traditional religious group may find community in one of the many specialized support groups we have today, such as Alcoholics Anonymous. The people in these twelve-step programs practice a sort of guerilla spirituality. You go to a meeting of one of these groups, and you pull up their britches, they have dragon bites all over them. These people do not just theorize about the great dragon. They have actually met the dragon, and it almost killed them, and they know it. They are serious. That is what makes them so much more authentic and serious than most other religious types. This kind of guerilla spirituality is why I admire them so much. It is an important part of what I call "street magic."

This is survival spirituality. These people know that you do not pray to be sweet and wonderful. If you are praying to be sweet and wonderful, then your prayer is just another part of your spiritual posturing, your inflation and grandiosity. No, you pray to deal effectively with this great dragon that is in the process of trying to devour you, because you know that in and of yourself you are not equal to it. People go to these meetings because they know they cannot solve the problem alone. If they leave, they know they will soon be tempted to fall off the wagon again. So they stay in touch with their group support for making the grandiosity conscious and keeping the dragon at bay.

The twelve-step concept of spirituality, to the extent that they don't try to secularize it, serves as a model for humanity to get serious about coping with the dragon of grandiosity. What we need is a group "Humans Anonymous."

Audience: There is something called "Co-Dependents Anonymous," a twelve-step program for people who want to get help with human relationships.

Moore: That can be useful too. All these twelve-step groups are a powerful ritual resource, because they help people bring their problems into consciousness. They often say, for example, "I am always going to be an alcoholic, and I need you people to help me deal with it." We need to reframe that, because it is the same thing as saying, "I am always going to have a problem with my grandiosity." People who cannot admit they have a permanent problem with their tendencies toward pathological grandiosity are simply deluding themselves, and they become part of the larger human problem. We all need to take part in a human recovery project. These programs provide good models for us for serious survival spirituality, for guerilla spirituality!

WORSHIP AND LITURGY

Another resource for regulating grandiose energies is regular participation in communal worship and liturgy. If we bracket the religious tribalism issue for a moment and focus on the individual's regulatory needs, then liturgy does offer a partial containment and regulation. Remember we are talking about marking time. It helps if you have a liturgical year to follow. Christians are not the only ones who have done that. Most people in the world before the modern era used sacred calendars to mark time and help them feel oriented in relation to a true center. They used this means to contain themselves and help themselves stay sane, to provide something predictable, a dependable structure for living.

Say, for example, that you are a borderline personality, and you don't have enough money to get the kind of therapy you need. You can at least go to Mass every morning. That regular ritual process can develop into a selfobject container that helps you regulate the radical volatility of your psyche. It is my experience working with borderlines, and other extremely unstructured people, that if they work along the outlines of a liturgical year, or work regularly through a liturgical process, it helps them avoid acting out and other self-destructive behaviors. It may not cure them, but it helps them contain their pathology. This applies to all of us, of course, not just to borderline personalities.

ANCIENT MAGICAL TECHNIQUES

Another way to help people remember that they are not God would be to rediscover the practical human ritual use of ancient magical techniques that were specieswide prior to modernization (Moore 2001). The use of talismans, for instance, is very simple. Consider the tangible ritual objects used by Roman Catholics through the centuries, the rosary and the crucifix. The Catholics made a mistake by deemphasizing the use of such techniques after Vatican II. You do not hear much about them anymore, but those objects are symbols that represent the archetypal Self, psychologically speaking. That is why Jung made the distinction between symbols and signs. Freudians do not have an adequate theory of symbolism, and they view all ritual practice as obsessional. A Jungian knows that a ritual symbol can help regulate archetypal energies when it symbolizes an affirmation by a person that the archetypal Self is not the ego.

Some mentally ill people have found that keeping a rosary in their pocket during the day helps restrain them from acting out destructively. They may reach into their pocket during a meeting and touch the rosary that has been blessed by some priest or nun with whom they feel a deep spiritual connection. I say this purely as a psychoanalyst now. I have yet to see any research to show me that such a habit is not helpful, particularly for severely ill people. I would like to see any research evidence that such a practice makes people crazier. It doesn't exist! Such practices help people regulate and limit their chaotic tendencies. This should not surprise us, because you only have to know a little history to know that human beings have always found such things helpful.

Consider, for example, all the current New Age talk about crystals and sacred stones. Having a sacred stone on your person is a very ancient practice. Why does it work? Because a stone archetypally carries the archetype of the Self. The philosopher's stone, *lapis,* is an image of God. When you touch the stone, you do not think the stone actually is God, but the stone participates in the being of God sacramentally, and it reminds you that God is there, and you are not alone. It becomes a "means of grace."[2] So the stone serves as yet another possible antidote for unconscious identification with the dragon and offers a soothing sense of connection to a great "other."

THE LIFE OF PRAYER

This recommendation of prayer is perhaps my most radical. I can just hear people gasping, "My God! Is a professional psychoanalyst going to recommend prayer?!" Yes, in fact, I am. It is amazing how many people in our secularized world start complaining the moment you bring up prayer as something that might help people deal with their pathological narcissism. People have been overwhelmed by the assumption, based primarily on Freudian biases and little else, certainly very little research, about how destructive prayer is. They assume that prayer makes people more compulsive than they were before, that prayer leads people toward schizophrenia. I want to see the research that supports such views. Show me the empirical research studies. There is, to the contrary, a burgeoning body of research that shows how prayer can be helpful in both emotional and physical health (see Dossey 1993, Dossey and Borysenko 1999, DeBlassie 1990).

People who have a regular prayer life ritual handle their compulsions and impulsivity better than those who do not. They are less fragmented than those who do not pray regularly. When you are talking with them, it is easier to disidentify with the king and queen within, even if you are not visualizing.

Personally, I prefer visualization. The commandment to "make no graven images" didn't mean you shouldn't try to visualize God. If you know how to do this, you don't make graven images, but you visualize them as they present themselves in visionary experience. Some people are obsessively Protestant about this and have a Protestant hermeneutic that claims it is bad to see God. That misreads the whole meaning of the deeper tradition. I'm a Protestant myself, so I can say these things. The Protestant protest was a revolt against literalism and idolatry, not against the use of imaginal resources in prayer.

Audience: How would you define prayer?

Moore: Prayer is any spiritual discipline that enables you to be connected with the basic energies of life and keeps you from an unconscious fantasy that you yourself are God or the God king or queen. Prayer is anything that enables you to disidentify with the God king or queen and yet remain connected to their life-giving energies. So if you hear me say, for example, that sexuality is prayer, that is what I mean, because if you are in true harmony with your body, you will not mistake yourself for the Godhead. You know you are a creature.

People sometimes say, "What about all those promiscuous people?" But promiscuous people are not actually in harmony with their bodies. Listen to the line in the musical *Les Misérables* where the prostitute says to the man, "You do not know that you are having sex with someone who is already dead." Crazy sexuality does not get acted out by someone who is in harmony with their body.

Audience: Can you distinguish between prayer and meditation?

Moore: I consider prayer any form of meditation that helps the human ego know it is not identical with the archetypal Self, for example, the Tibetan Buddhist *tankas,* the prayer images. I would consider meditation on a *tanka* as prayer. I agree with the Tibetans when they put up a prayer wheel and call it prayer. When they see the wind blowing the wheel, they say that is prayer. I agree that it is prayer if you understand it.

In my own consulting room, I keep images that I can see with my peripheral vision to remind me of God in different traditions, to remind me that I am not the center. I do not have to say a thing. All I have to do is be aware in my peripheral vision of that image and it reminds me that I am a creature. So it helps me deal with any idealizing transferences that might tend to stimulate my grandiosity and tempt me to claim ownership of the dragon energy.

Certain forms of meditation teach you to focus on some mandala or other external center that lies outside the individual. However, those forms that make you think you are "the great one" can be very dangerous for some people. If you start depersonalizing and start merging into "the great one," you may become psychotic. Some forms of meditation can loosen your connection to a nonego center. You have to look carefully to see whether any particular practice actually helps the ego deal with grandiosity. Some of them do, some of them do not.

We have not explored these areas enough. Only now are we finding psychotherapists who know enough history of religions and anthropology to begin to look at the whole use of objects, of rituals, of gift-giving, things we were taught were dangerous. Only now are we beginning to educate a group of therapists informed enough and bold enough to take a fresh look at these things for potential use in healing ritualization.

VISIONS OF THE OTHER WORLD, PARADISE,
AND THE LIFE BEYOND

Audience: I believe it was Marx who said rather cynically that religion is the opiate of the masses, and in a sense, he was right.

Moore: Certainly. Religion in some of its forms tends to be more destructive in some places than in others. Some kinds of religious fundamentalism that legitimate your inflation against other people can cause a destructive acting out. Religion itself, however, is clearly psychoactive. Jungians understand religion in a very different way than did Marx and Freud and the traditional Freudians.

Audience: Do you think the notion of a literal hereafter has been destructive? Should we consider heaven a destructive "pie in the sky"?

Moore: There is a lot of talk about that. I personally tend to be an empiricist who considers what actually happens to people with these various points of view. For example, some of my students minister in African-American churches where some of the members might have less energy and incentive for the struggles of this world if they did not believe in a literal hereafter. My guess is that belief in "the other world," the homeland, probably gives many people more courage to deal with this world, rather than giving them less courage and thus weakening them. I know that many people say it weakens us, but I have not personally seen any proof for that statement, and I do not believe it.

Audience: Even if some people need it, how can you get them enthused about the idea of preserving this planet when they have better things waiting for them in heaven?

Moore: Tillich would say that one can participate in history and time in a fragmentary experience of the fulfillment of eternity. Such a partial, anticipatory participation can fuel courage and action now in anticipation of an eschatological great celebration when the prodigal children all come to a great homecoming.

In the processes of prayer and active imagination, you do not necessarily have to visualize the king and queen in a literal, physical place called heaven. Some might say they are in mythic sacred geography, and others might think they are "no place at all." I prefer that people rediscover their imaginal mythic consciousness. Like Joseph Campbell, I suggest people get their own myths going and operating and having imaginal access, as Robert Bly (1990) says, to "the other world." Bly is a poet, and he can get away with it. Perhaps we should all just forget about theology and become poets.

No matter how you conceptualize it, practically speaking we still must talk to the king and the queen in the other world. We need to establish contact and make this relationship an inner mythic reality.

But back to the issue of how it effects courage to face this world. Does knowledge of a homeland with a king and queen in it make you less hopeful or more hopeful? It depends on many other factors. It might make some people less hopeful, but that is not my experience in working with people. My experience is that once people have some sense of a king and queen in the other world, they tend to be calmer and work harder. I have never investigated whether they were working hard to get there, or whether they were working hard just because they wanted to serve their king and queen. Perhaps I will start asking my students and analysands, "Are you doing these things because you want to go and be with the king and queen after you get through here in this life? Or is it just because you want to be faithful to your inner king and queen?" Check in with me in a few years, and I will tell you what they said.

Audience: Mario Jacoby has a book called *Longing for Paradise* (1985) that traces the archetypal root of the desire for a hereafter.

Moore: Certainly there is an archetypal root, but we must ask how it helps us regulate our energy and anxiety. It has probably evolved because it was useful to our species in the "struggle for survival."

CREATING MYTH FOR TODAY

What we need is not more demythologization, but *re-mythologization*. We need to play with myth and get it out of this academic idiom. We need to ask, "What would an adequate planetary myth be like, one that would adequately contain us as a human family?" We need some serious play about that. So I recommend to people that they start writing myths. Why don't individual people just start writing their myths and sharing them with others? Write myths that might be adequate for the whole human family. Experiment and draw upon your own mythic resources. That is what I would like to see people do.

Why do we have to have a homecoming? Isn't this just a Heideggerian fantasy? The answer to that is "why *shouldn't* we have a homecoming myth of how we go back and reconnect with the king and the queen, of how all of us prodigal children can go home together?" We can have all kinds of psychologically helpful myths. You can work with myth until you find the way it feels right for you, extending the same privilege to others, of course. Then, if you care, you can ask the theologians to deal with the myth later. If they cannot do it in a helpful way, then you do not need to waste your time with them.

According to Eliade, people need to have an image of a homeland. That is a myth. We do have a classic myth of a homeland, the story of Ulysses in the *Odyssey*, Homer's epic poem. It is a universal human myth that there is a homeland.

You can work with ontology and metaphysics and theology if you wish, but it is also useful and fun to play with these inner mythic realities and go exploring within yourself. Maybe you will come back and tell us something important from which we can all benefit. Perhaps we should have a contest to write the best science fiction screenplay for the film "Close Encounters of the Fourth Kind: The Human Journey Home." That would address this deep longing within us.

Most important of all, however, to come full circle, we must get all this mythic numinous god-energy contained and into mythic vessels. Then we can work together on bringing it back in creative and useful forms. Together we must create in imagination an adequate inner temple, an effective chalice, the true Holy Grail. Because until we do, we will continue to cannibalize and destroy the earth!

If anyone can figure out how to solve this problem without reclaiming myth, please let me know. This is why Joseph Campbell's work continues to be so popular and powerful. People sense they need myth to contain and enact these archetypal longings in a healthy way. This is undoubtedly also the reason for the resurgence today in the popularity of storytelling. We have storytelling festivals. Why not myth-sharing festivals?

So we all need to sit around the global campfire once again and tell stories to each other, tell people what is happening. With people sitting around the campfire, and the fire burning away, we can say, "Okay, what have you heard about what is happening over in the homeland?" So the ritual elders, the people who perhaps are better storytellers than the others, will say, "I understand that such and such is happening in the homeland." It is like that line in the play *Camelot,* "I wonder what the king is doing tonight." It is that same type of mythic imagination. It may be play, but it is "high play." If we will do it, not only will our children love it, but our species might begin to awake from its long sleep and repetitive nightmares.

The next chapter presents a summary of practical tactics for facing the dragon of grandiosity. This list continues to grow daily, however, and readers may be able to think of some that I have not included. I will welcome hearing your suggestions as I begin work on the sequel to this book.

NOTES

1. This chapter is an edited account of part of the late morning session on Sunday, July 16, 1989, of a weekend workshop and discussion led by Robert Moore at the C. G. Jung Institute in Chicago, Illinois. The original program was entitled "Jungian Psychology and Human Spirituality: Liberation from Tribalism in Religious Life."
2. On the role of symbols in mediating the sacramental reality of the spiritual presence, see Paul Tillich, *Systematic Theology* (1957), vol. 3.

CHAPTER 11

Dragon Laws

Insights for Confronting Grandiosity

FREUD INTRODUCED THE CONCEPT OF INEXORABLE LAWS of the psyche that operate without the ego's knowledge or cooperation. In his articulation of the "law of the talion," the *lex talionis,* the unconscious always "keeps score." Whenever this unconscious entity perceives an injustice or other grievance, it starts an implacable process that seeks redress, often in horrifying ways.

Freud's insight fits well into a comprehensive understanding of the dynamics of the unconscious. This chapter uses a series of "dragon laws" to summarize the introductory fundamentals of these dynamics and their implications for personal, social, and spiritual life.

Earlier chapters discussed in depth what is at stake in our capacity to wake up and face the dragon. Not facing our own unconscious grandiose god-energies keeps us from the creative challenge of "riding the dragon": becoming a conscious partner of the archetypal Great Self Within and thereby moving toward our optimum best selves.

We need the help of dragon energies to move toward a more radiant life, and the first step in getting that help is to awaken ourselves to their presence and relate to them consciously. The sequel to this volume, *Riding the Dragon,* will delve more deeply into what must follow after we become aware of the dragon's omnipresence in our lives; here we address the paramount need to achieve the initial consciousness.

Remaining unconscious of the dragon's presence would insure that we spend most if not all of our waking hours experiencing what Paul Tillich called "existential estrangement" from our best, optimum potential selves. In traditional mythic language, unconsciousness of the dragon's presence invokes a Satan complex that mobilizes within us as an adversary to our own conscious ego. We guarantee, in effect, that we will live "in hell" without knowing consciously where and how we made that choice. We usually have no idea how it was that our unconsciousness served as a portal for this satanic energy to enter into our families, our communities, and the world in general.

The starkness of this choice has a terrible simplicity: you can either become conscious or stay unconscious of the reality and presence of the dragon. This great turn from being asleep at the wheel to an alert knowing of the powerful proximity of the great Other is the most important gnosis you can ever possess about your personal, social, or spiritual life.

The "dragon laws" that follow review and summarize how to awaken to the presence of the dragon and then contain and channel its energy.

DRAGON LAWS IN PERSONAL LIFE

We must always begin with the assumption that the dragon of grandiosity is present and awake within us. The question is not, "Is there any grandiosity in me?" but "*Where* are my grandiose energies manifesting without my being aware of them? If I am aware of them, do I disrespectfully think and act as if I own them?"

1. To the extent that you are not aware of the dragon's presence, it is already manifesting in a satanic or Luciferian complex in your personality, usually without your being aware of it.

The first absolutely essential task is to become aware of its presence and start watching for signs of its mercurial manifestations. These signs usually don't seem dramatic enough to be detected, so we must use the creative trickster of our inner magus to penetrate the cloaking mechanisms which, as Freud knew, are really defenses of the ego against knowing its real situation.

2. We either identify with this inner complex of grandiose energies, or we repress it and project it onto others.

People who identify with them tend to use them with arrogance and disrespect. Those who try to deny them tend to idealize others and give away their sovereignty and power, leading to envy and hate.

3. In actual experience, the ego can oscillate between the poles of identification and projection, thus creating a cycle between (a) inflation and arrogance and (b) projection, idealization, and demonization.

We need to begin a careful scrutiny that scans for telltale signs of where grandiose energy is entering into our personality and daily lives. Since it is a shapeshifter, we must comb through our experience carefully to discern the shapes it took when we were unaware of its presence.

My research found four primary archetypal forms or shapes that dragon energies unconsciously take: royal energy of the king and queen, warrior energy, magician or magus energy, and lover energy.

4. **Dragon energy manifested in the royal archetype exhibits its grandiosity through the ego's posturing and pretension to be more in control of things than it really is.**

You experience the nagging anxiety and ontological emptiness that underlies the pretense of running things and being the center. You may be addicted to the idealizing projections of other people, so that when they refuse to idealize you, you nervously feel your anxiety more intensely.

The royal form seeks to maximize hierarchical control and domination over others. Our ego says we do this "for their own good." In its sociopathic form (what Theodore Millon (1969) calls an "active independent" form), you think that you are the law and other people are here only to do your will. When such persons become paranoid, as they usually do, their behavior insures that they will have good reasons for their paranoia. This is the royal form of dragon hell.

5. **Dragon energy manifested in the warrior archetype shows its grandiosity in workaholism, the fantasy that you can keep the world from crashing down around your ears by working harder and harder.**

You may also get compulsive rage energy expressed in bullying, physical and verbal aggression, and violent fantasies and behavior. You rationalize the rage with your conviction that you are one of the righteous ones defending the cosmos against evil. This fantasy gives you the role of a sinless and righteous avenger assigned to bring down divine wrath on the demonic ones. Your own grandiosity is not available to your consciousness but is carried by your perceived enemy. This enables you to act without empathy, compassion, or love.

This madness of grandiose warrior acting out must be confronted and contained, whether the perpetrator is a violent husband, a terrorist, or nation engaging in aggression, oppression, or genocide. When possessed by warrior grandiosity, however, whether in the family, in police work, or in military actions, one always seeks to express as much unnecessary force as one can muster in the situation. This is the erotic, sadomasochistic, necrophilic appeal of savage violent acting out that classical Freudian psychoanalysts tried to help us face and confront, unfortunately without much success to date. This is the warrior form of dragon hell.

> **6. Dragon energy manifested in the magician or magus archetype causes you to be strangely emotionally detached, "above it all."**

You think you have the right, correct, enlightened point of view (theory, ideology, theology, psychology, or spiritual tradition), and that if people would accept your version of truth (doctrine, theory, ideology, or tradition), then everything would be okay. The now-integrated spirituality of an enlightened and peaceful world would easily see that evil is no more than an illusion held by those still unenlightened but marginal people who don't know what you know.

Magician grandiosity cloaks a fundamental coldness, a lack of love and joy, and a denial of the horror of radical evil. With the erroneous perception that you are above it, you try to avoid any responsibility for confronting it. You keep telling yourself that the horrible things happening in the world are just illusions, that the world can only be improved by accepting your version of the truth. Only the abstract theoretical correctness of your belief system will suffice.

This fantasy allows you to reject any notion of cooperating with others in urgently needed programs of compassion and justice. You see no need for a calm, centered, and blessing presence in the midst of all the chaos in family, community, nation, and planet. You see no need for joyful, embodied celebration of the preciousness of individual people. You see no need for wedding feasts, ecstatic erotic unions, messianic banquets, or sacramental dances of life, for all these things require repulsive engagement with particular real people. Surely humanity can be redeemed without all that messiness! This is the magician form of dragon hell.

7. **Dragon energy manifested in the lover archetype makes you believe that the world begins and ends with your feelings, your pain, and your bodily and emotional needs.**

Your victimization becomes the most important thing in the world. You are helpless in this weakened state, so no one should expect you to care about anyone else's needs. Your needs are greater, and people don't give them the importance they deserve. If they did, they would drop everything else and get busy meeting your needs for food, sex, comfort, recognition, status, prestige, economic support, and so on.

Your ego has always longed for the experience of happiness to get beyond its shame and find meaningful sexual expression and satisfying intimacy with others, but unconscious grandiosity has brought you more despair and toxic shame than happiness, and

sexuality is either numb, greedy, or addictive. Flooding lover energy pushes you into substance abuse, depression, codependent or
masochistic patterns of intimate relationships, or destructive idealization of others, leaving you feeling passive and dependent.

Everyone else is at fault for this but you. They created this hell
you are living in, and they should work to get you out of it. If they
were really adequate and responsible, they would liberate you from
your pain and suffering by providing you with more food, nar-
cotics, sex, money, and status. They have all the gold, but they're
just hoarding it. If they were really good people, they would give it
to you, because you deserve it. This is the lover form of dragon hell.

These examples show how dragon energies use trickster creativity to insert themselves into our experience when we try to stay
ignorant of their presence. A little study helps one get better at rec-
ognizing the various disguises. Any one of these unconscious ways
of expressing dragon energy can bring chaos into your life and
make it a living hell. Lack of awareness allows us to become por-
tals through which hell can find its way into our lives. To become
aware of how the dragon is invading or colonizing your life and
forcing you into one of the circles of hell without your realizing it,
you need to learn how to recognize dragon signs. You can prepare
yourself to be a scout for yourself and others.

8. **The various shapes of unconscious grandiosity have
   some dragon signs in common, such as chronic anxiety,
   despair, hopelessness, aimlessness, lack of a sense of limits, lack of a sense of mystery, emotional coldness rang-
   ing from detachment to hate, and a lack of empathy,
   compassion, or joy.**

These marks indicate that the dragon is very close, no matter
what stealthy form it might be taking. So long as its presence

remains unconscious, the positive counterparts of these marks cannot manifest in an adequate way.

    9. Only by consciously and respectfully facing the dragon's presence and responding in faith to "the great other" can we manifest the positive signs, what Tillich called "the fruits of the spiritual presence": love, hope, peace, joy, courage, gnosis and wisdom, and passion for justice.

Many spiritual traditions have used the term *repentance* for consciously awakening to our grandiosity, confronting our psychological and spiritual idolatry, and changing our fundamental attitude and direction. Whatever we call it, without such a change, we will stay lost in despair and mired in estrangement from ourselves, from others, and from nature.

    10. The fabric of what Tillich called our "dreaming innocence" is torn when the enchantment of malignant unknowing has been pierced by the first epiphany of awareness of the reality and presence of the dragon.

We become aware, perhaps for the first time, that we have not been so innocent after all. We suddenly start feeling empathy for others who live in their own self-maintained, creative versions of the dragon's hell and act out their own misery and fraudulent self-righteousness in destructive attitudes and behaviors. Without the illusion of innocence, we more readily understand why they do the things they do. We note with surprise the beginnings of compassion being born within us, even for those who do those things we find terrible. By finally saying "yes" to the truth that our unconscious knew all along, we see new psychological and spiritual fruits of the spirit being born in us and around us.

But what about our anxiety? Doesn't knowing this terrible truth about ourselves make it worse? On the contrary. The wisest psychotherapists with the most experience on the "road less traveled" agree on this with the spiritual masters of every great tradition. When we consciously face our hidden superiority complex, our preening sense of entitlement, enlightenment, and self-righteousness, then we can escape our delusional claim to be helpless victims, and our anxieties mysteriously begin to diminish.

> 11. **Anxiety declines as unconscious grandiosity declines.**

> 12. **Denying our creaturehood causes the truth to return to us as symptoms in our body and psyche.**

The more unconscious grandiosity we have, the more anxiety we experience in our body. Recent research in neurophysiology confirms the physical nature of anxiety, how it floods the body with toxic hormones and neurotransmitters that attack the body's supply of life energy and its capacity to defend and repair itself. When we attend to our embodiment as creatures, and treat our bodies with empathy and compassion, this affirmation of creaturehood counteracts our grandiosity and lowers our anxiety. We must attend to our need for deep breathing, centering prayer and meditation, and start facing life tasks with more focused problem-solving behavior. (This explains why the techniques described in chapter 10 are so helpful.)

Prayer and active imagination also work with the creative and supportive face of the dragon to provide dragon energy and dragon insight. You have more insight into what you must change, and you have more energy to fuel the courage you will need to continue the transformative process.

The inner magician also works better as your anxiety comes

down. You listen better, focus better, think clearer, and engage in more effective, down-to-earth problem-solving behavior. Where you previously were a legend in your own mind and sole possessor of answers to all the world's problems, you now find that you can balance your checkbook! The decline of magician grandiosity makes possible a new advent of wisdom into your personality. Now you can pick up a book like Stephen Covey's *Seven Habits of Highly Effective People* (1989) and start putting its wisdom and insightful techniques to use.

Increased effectiveness will allow you to access your warrior energies in a more creative way. It was unconscious warrior grandiosity that led you to think you could live successfully without engaging in detailed and focused problem-solving. Trying to solve real problems turns off the panic, fear, and anxiety switches in your brain. This improves your ability to listen, think, and assess situations wisely. *In short, as unconscious grandiosity declines, your actual effectiveness and creative productivity increase.*

A key transformation occurs when you reach a certain point in the centering and calming process. You can begin to access your royal dragon energies in a creative and healing way that embodies what systems theorists call a "calm, non-anxious presence," the *sine qua non* for effective leadership in family, community, nation, or planet.

When grandiose lover energies become more conscious and respectfully regulated, we put more value on other people and curb our longings to merge with them. Our sexual activity includes more tenderness and genuine empathy for the partner. Appetites transform from compulsion to an appreciative consciousness with enhanced awareness of the presence of the beautiful. Best of all, the increasing calmness enables us to slow down and "smell the flowers," opening up a deep new sense of joy that can be nurtured to permeate all aspects of our experience. Here, more than anywhere else, we realize that we have opened a portal for some heavenly energies to enter into our lives.

DRAGON LAWS IN SOCIAL LIFE

These principles have many implications for social and cultural relationships. Once awakened from the "dreaming innocence" of unconscious grandiosity, we move decisively to establish our attitudinal and behavioral assumptions on a foundation of respect, empathy, and compassion, and this leads to better opportunities for reconciliation and creative cooperation.

13. **Unconscious grandiosity is the fundamental psychological engine behind our lack of respect and empathy for people who do not share our social location.**

It is the main engine of racism, classism, sexism, malignant nationalism, and terrorism. When dragon energies are present unconsciously, we have little concern for even the most blatant inequities. Injustice is not high on our list of concerns. We look for ways to stay in denial, to rationalize our acceptance of poverty, disease, political oppression, and environmental despoilation. Our "let them eat cake" attitude ignores the degradation and despair in refugee camps all over the world. We have no time to cooperate with compassionate action on behalf of people who cannot help themselves.

We declare our lack of interest in nation-building among the abandoned, dispossessed, the "wretched of the earth." In deference to so-called national security, we engage in the grandiose fantasy that we can live safely inside our gated communities while children elsewhere die of starvation and treatable diseases in the laps of their emaciated mothers. Thus the grandiose attitudes and behaviors of rich and powerful nations help create a fertile soil for extremism in the poor and weak ones.

Young people are tempted by despair when they see their kinsmen in such appalling conditions. They become easy prey for articulate, charismatic demagogues who promise them a more decisive and heroic leadership than that offered by their ostensible but ineffectual elders. Warrior brotherhoods that are malignantly tribal and flamboyantly grandiose rise up to bear the "divine wind" of retribution to the enemy. Their hate and rage displaces all remnants of human compassion and empathy, even for noncombatants. The psychodynamics behind the rise of Osama bin Laden's terrorist network are the same as those at work in the German Nazis and fanatical Japanese warrior cults of the 1930s.

> 14. Grandiose, disrespectful, and unempathic behavior by people with social and political power always generates powerful, rage-filled compensatory outbreaks of madness.

Such behavior is fueled by a despair that feels powerless and has little or nothing to lose. In lieu of hope for a future on earth, a heroic death becomes intoxicatingly attractive.

The ancient Greek wisdom that *hubris* (pride) inexorably leads to *nemesis* (retribution) has been substantiated by every spiritual tradition. Concern for nemesis is more than a paranoid worry of a few people "soft-minded" about spirituality. Whatever one's attitude about religion, the arrogant dismissal of the reality of retribution carries a high price. The greater the grandiosity, the higher the price, and tragically, not just to the arrogant. There is almost always some terrible collateral damage. Horrific lose-lose scenarios of rageful escalations are typical of our species. We must find a better way.

15. Finding a better way will require us to learn how to discern the signs of the unconscious grandiose energies in our social groups and their leaders.

This is never easy, because investing our grandiosity in sociocultural groups was how we avoided facing our own personal grandiosity in the first place. Systems theorists claim that all social groups systemically resist all attempts to change them and their characteristic attitudes and behaviors. So when we try to challenge the grandiosity of our social group and bring its shadow into the light, we can expect that we will come under attack. The greater the challenge, the greater the attack. Only by standing with courage in our awakened state can we hope to be agents of transformation, reconciliation, and healing in our social world.

DRAGON LAWS AND SPIRITUAL LIFE

The dragon of unconscious grandiosity roams freely in the attitudes and behaviors of all spiritual traditions and their devotees. Pervasive religious grandiosity and unwitting, consciously well-intentioned idolatry provide an equal opportunity seduction for the spiritually inclined of all tribes. It is easy to mask prodigious amounts of personal grandiosity as a weak and selfless humility once you have displaced your grandiose energies onto your spiritual tribe.

16. Spiritual grandiosity usually issues in grandiose claims for the mandate of one's own spiritual tribe under the assumed aegis of divine reality.

The original conscious intent was simply to work one small part of the divine plan, but the seductive dragon of narcissistic grandiosity soon convinces us that we are the divine plan. The arrogant, exhibitionistic presentation of intuitions or revelations that one tribe has special and exclusive divine approval is one of the most common ways for the energies of hell to be channeled into human history. All spiritual tribes and their devotees are subject to this tendency to believe in their own marketing and to see themselves as legends in their own minds.

> 17. Such naïve exclusivistic claims to know the divine mind ignores the invariable limitations of human thought and the limitations of mythic and symbolic language in discerning the divine mysteries (see Tillich 1957).

All spiritual traditions and their leaders, without exception, are susceptible to the tempting seduction of turning the symbols that mediated the divine presence to them into idols that block the light.

> 18. Every powerful manifestation or appearance of the sacred (hierophany or epiphany) tends to become imperialistic in the hands of its more "spiritually challenged" interpreters (see Eliade 1959).

Unfortunately, not all stewards of tradition are, like Moses, competent magi. When Moses touched the rock, living water came forth. When incompetent ones do the interpreting, the fruit is more like that of the sorcerer's apprentice, for it brings hell into the world instead of living water or true bread.

> 19. Those who have no empathy for other people currently misinterpreting their own traditions are likely to be unconscious of their own grandiose claims to exclusive entitlement.

Alfred Adler provided the painful truth of this insight. Jewish, Christian, and Islamic traditions have all struggled with this seduction, with each one pointing its finger at the others and denouncing them as bogus pretenders to the role of "the elect" or true people of God.

While most traditions have a sense of the true spiritual warrior and the reality of spiritual warfare against radical evil, not all traditions are equally as vulnerable to the seduction of literalizing a so-called holy war against other spiritual tribes. All traditions know in their mystical core that the true *jihad* is a struggle against their own idolatry, especially the desire to replace the authentically divine with the ego's pretentious and self-serving interpretations.

> 20. The so-called peoples of the book in the Abrahamic traditions of Judaism, Christianity, and Islam are particularly tempted toward literalizing and acting out their sense of special election in violent ways.

These claims historically have not been just to a place in heaven, but made to justify appropriating the lands of other people and then refusing to share with them the bounty of the earth in peace, prosperity, and mutual affection. We will know that the peoples of the book have faced this shared issue when they start working together to solve the problem of the Holy City of Jerusalem. It should be clear that political authority over Jerusalem itself is not the real problem. The spiritual grandiosity of all parties involved is the real obstacle to a peaceful cooperative solution.

But what if your intuition or revelation about the specialness of your tribe in the unfolding of the divine plan is actually true in some mysterious way? Such a truth can never be literal or simplistic, because we all know that creatures only "see through a glass darkly." Once you realize how easy it is to be narcissistically wounded and thus feel inferior and insignificant, you will see that arrogantly trumpeting your privileged position to other tribes results from your own unconscious grandiosity, the satanic Lucifer complex.

> 21. **People who truly awake to the divine presence and power in their tradition do not need to trumpet their privileges.**

Once you truly "offer up" your unconscious grandiosity on the tribal altar, the light of your tribe will so shine that the authenticity of your election and special role will be evident and impressive to everyone without your having to explain it to them. One legend says that the messianic banquet will feast on the body of the great dragon Leviathan. This legend could well come true if enough people would begin to offer up their unconscious grandiosity as a sacrifice to the real spiritual presence. The light of the tribe would then shine brightly in its works of empathy, love, and compassion, in its effective care for those people who have no other advocates or resources.

The attempt to turn the divine presence into an exclusive franchise has been the historic tragedy of all religious tribes, without exception, from the fundamentalists of the right to the fundamentalists of the left. Even those who assume the mantle of "most liberal and tolerant" often use their ideological, hermeneutical, and political correctness to justify self-righteous posturing.

> 22. **Such grandiose spiritual posturing always markets itself as a commitment to transforming the world toward the reign of God on earth, but it is actually an "ego-spirituality."**

The cup is full of self and cannot experience the openness that leaves room for authentic empathy or compassion for others.

23. People standing in unconscious spiritual grandiosity, anxious to be idealized by others, are particularly reactive to any lack of dogmatic or ideological agreement.

Their narcissism demands a rigid ideological sameness from everyone. They experience the unique interpretations of others as painful narcissistic wounds to their own inflated pretensions, and this provokes a whole constellation of rage responses. They see "the other" as a demonic agent shaking the foundations of their already shaky narcissistic equilibrium. They see their own unconscious satanic inflation in the face of "the other." They generate unconscious genocidal fantasies of holy revenge. They want to become heroes who step up to the task of cleansing the world of chaos and evil. The prospect of performing rituals of sacred violence against "the other" begins to glow with archetypal energy in their unconscious.

24. A severe enough narcissistic wound causes unconscious fantasies to irrupt into the consciousness for acting out.

Possessed individuals hijack the symbols of their tradition to rationalize and channel the emerging compulsive necrophilic and nihilistic energy and behavior, so they can be demonically creative without becoming personally chaotic, planning and executing acts of mass murder, so to speak, with a clear conscience.

Why shouldn't you be so creative? Like Faust, you can channel the hideous strength of satanic energies into the purity of your hatred. This is how Hitler's elite S.S. corps, Hirohito's samurai, and bin Laden's Al-Quaeda all became so terrifyingly effective in their missions of hate and destruction.

Without a powerful awakening in our species, we will no doubt see more of these gifted Jedi knights going over to the dark side of the Force. Where are the Jedi knights who are not possessed by this kind of satanic enchantment?

> 25. Leaders in every spiritual tribe must face the urgent task of asking how their own grandiose attitudes and behaviors are blocking the light that needs to shine more than ever now that history has reached this critical time with so much potential for a great turning.

As in personal and social life, the question is not whether my spiritual tribe is grandiose, but *"How* is my spiritual tribe grandiose? How does it manifest the presence of the dragon energies in an unconscious way? Where is the hidden grandiosity?"

Spiritual tribes show their unconscious grandiosity most clearly by their reluctance to engage enthusiastically and effectively in cooperative deeds of compassion that build a common future habitat for humanity and its friends. The relative grandiosity of any spiritual tribe or organization can be discerned by the degree to which it sets aside its claims of exclusive superiority and steps instead into bold, cooperative, and compassionate action with other tribes to meet the needs of the poor, the hungry, the imprisoned, the oppressed.

> 26. When a tribe's spiritual grandiosity declines, it immediately gains more radiance as a portal for the incarnation in history of what Tillich called the "authentic spiritual community."

This community is made up of individuals from all spiritual tribes, and it even includes some who do not identify themselves with any tribe, yet still embody in a mysterious way the transformative presence of the true spirit that is above every name. Entry into this radiant spiritual community only requires an authentic and effective confrontation with the existential and psychological, if not theological, idolatry that represents the attempt to substitute human ego for divine reality.

How can we know that this authentic spiritual community is present in the work of any tribe? Once we face the dragon of our spiritual grandiosity and open ourselves up to awareness of the spiritual presence, miracles begin to happen in us and around us (Tillich 1957). The fruits of the presence of the true spirit begin to manifest with amazing forcefulness and clarity. Love suddenly arrives with more power, and the romance of hate and rage begins to lose its enchanting power. Anxiety and fear rapidly begin to decline. We suddenly find ourselves able to cooperate effectively with some unlikely people in doing the right things. Courage enables us to take a stand both for our best selves and for a world of justice and peace. We lose our blindness to the beauty that was around us all along, and we begin to experience joy!

When we are privileged to witness the presence of great goodness in people and communities during terrible times like the aftermath of September 11th, something radical, decisive, and irreversible changes within us. We remember something that our enchanted sleep had let slip away from us. Although we grieve about all the waste and the nightmare of our human past and present personal and collective grandiosity, when we witness a responsive outburst of courage, love, sacrifice, and generosity, it makes us doubt our despair and cynicism, and begin to look for ways to make things better.

Suddenly it is possible once again to entertain the thought that "Earth might be fair!" With Gandalf in Tolkien's *Return of the King*, we can say, "Come, there is much that we can yet do!" To prepare for a mission of effective transformative love, compassion, and healing in this struggling world, we will look for the courage to learn how to ride the dragon. That is our continuing project!

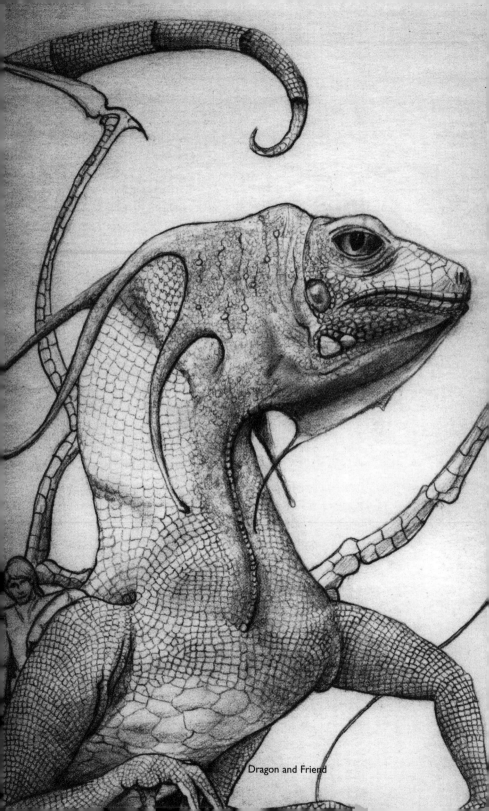

Dragon and Friend

CHAPTER 12

Beyond the Lucifer Complex

Befriending the Dragon

P REVIOUS CHAPTERS DISCUSSED THE IMPORTANT PROBLEMS
and issues that arise when we accept the task of facing
the dragon of psychological and spiritual grandiosity. In
conclusion, let me recap the main points and point the way to the
next agenda.

The widespread presence of dragon symbolism and imagery in
world mythology, both East and West, resulted from a general
intuition of the presence and dynamic power of a "great self"
within every human psyche that I call the "Great Self Within."
Psychoanalytic theorists like Freud, Adler, Jung, and Kohut all
referred to such a psychological reality, but with different names.
Freud called it the "id" and the "punitive superego," Adler called
it the "superiority complex" and the "depreciation tendency,"
Jung called it the "archetypal Self," and Kohut called it "grandiose
exhibitionistic self organization" and "narcissistic personality disorder." My own neo-Jungian psychoanalytic theory draws upon
all these theorists but attempts to document with more detailed
clarity the structure and dynamics of how the Great Self Within
expresses itself as grandiosity in our everyday psychological and
spiritual life.

This great force in the psyche is characterized by grandiose energies that constantly pressure the human ego from within, resulting in anxiety, mania, and depression. It generates two kinds of inflation: (a) personal, psychological, and spiritual states of possession and (b) idealizing projections that displace the grandiose energies onto other persons, institutions, or tribes expressed as religion, race, gender, social class, and so on. When we project grandiosity onto others to displace it from ourselves, the onset of chaos is only delayed and shifted to another more insidious form of expression. Much scapegoating and projective hate and ritual violence result, as was often characteristic of premodern peoples. Their ritual strategies, however, while morally flawed from our standpoint, were more sophisticated and effective than those currently being employed as cultures all over the world lose their traditional mythic and ritual vessels for limiting the freedom of the dragon.

In the wake of the modern eclipse of the mythic imagination and ritual process, the more recent strategy has been simply to deny the existence and power of the dragon and to attempt to function without a conscious awareness of its presence and power. As many of our spiritual and mythological traditions have intuited, when the darkness of such a malignant unknowing comes, the dragon can operate freely without detection. Then it can devour the consciousness and turn us into greedy, violent monsters bringing chaos and destruction that leads to fragmentation in our personalities and communities and to alienation and violence between the various spiritual traditions and tribes.

Premodern tribes were aware of this dragon's presence and power, and they put much of their energy into coping with its reality. A great deal of the intellectual energies and cultural creativity of premodern peoples went into gaining knowledge about how to deal with the reality and power of such transpersonal energies.

This led to elaborate systems of myth and ritual practice that attempted to connect with these transpersonal, ego-alien, sacred dragon energies and protect themselves from them.

Lacking the resources of depth psychology, however, even their most sophisticated understandings of the sacred energies in both good and demonic forms continued to rely heavily on mechanisms of externalization and projection. *This is why we must cease idealizing tribal shamanic and other premodern spiritual traditions.*

Even when they were aware of an "enemy within," they assumed that it came from an alien source of contamination, not from their own inner archetypal plumbing. The human ego, not yet completely possessed by the dragon, can experience its ego-alien nature, but it has difficulty seeing that it comes from the inner depths and not simply from outside. Before psychoanalysis, it was extremely difficult to understand that neither the problem nor the potential of dragon energies come "from out there."

Some of our human forebears intuited that the presence of dragon energies could be dangerous, and they determined to become enemies of the dragon. This "Ahab approach" occurs especially in Western traditions and is well illustrated in the stories of Beowulf and *Moby Dick.* The heroic ego is constantly surprised to find that the dragon keeps coming back, that it is very hard to kill.

People in modern times seem to be increasingly blind to the presence of the dragon and yet increasingly enchanted by its seductive power. The enchantment leads us to become increasingly destructive of both ourselves and our environment. Most people try to deny its reality and presence, while a few heroes try to kill it through psychoanalysis or cure it through various other techniques. Spiritual parallels are found in those techniques that seek to escape, whether through asceticism or renunciation, into a naïve "angelism" that seems to cultivate humility and inner peace. These psychological and spiritual approaches make elaborate systems of defense that deny the depth and difficulty of the continuing problem.

Such strategies are doomed to failure. The resourceful trickster capacities of the human psyche have a creative plethora of defense mechanisms that enable the ego to pretend that grandiosity is not present and not a problem. If denial is attempted and the ego unconsciously identifies with the grandiosity, then dangerous personal inflation results that expresses itself in one of the four forms delineated in my research.

More often the ego uses the unconscious mechanisms of projection and displacement to fend off the destabilizing personal effects of the grandiose energies and attempts to cope by displacing the grandiose energies onto relational, social, and religious vessels. Both grandiosity and true greatness are displaced through projective mechanisms and then both loved and hated in the ambivalent dance of idealization and envy.

When the grandiosity is displaced onto a group, the ego can experience less anxiety and feel righteous and humble while sanctioning horrific, arrogant, and hegemonic behaviors by the tribe. The Spanish Inquisition was a prime example of this all too popular human tactic. The long history of religious, ideological, and genocidal warfare exposes this failed strategy of coming to terms with the dragon energies within. We turn our arrogant inflation over to social, religious, ideological, institutional, or national surrogates, while our deep intuitions about the presence of an enemy cause us to demonize and dehumanize those other people outside our group.

Those people who think they have destroyed or mastered the dragon must look again. They are simply in a trickster trance, and it is having its way. Like Beowulf, they will have to face it again.

There is another strategy for dealing with the reality and power of the dragon that views it as the source of all creativity and blessing. When we relate to the dragon energies consciously and with respect, then individuals and the community at large can benefit from a positive relationship based on respectful good will and cooperation.

Carl Jung encountered cultural traditions embodying this alternative in his studies, most notably in his examination of Chinese culture. It is in this tradition of Jung that we find hope for a truly effective postmodern strategy for relating to the dragon. Both Carl Jung and Edward Edinger image for us the possibility of developing a conscious and respectful relationship with the presence and power of the archetypal Self, the Great Self Within, a relationship that can provide the human personality with inspiration, creative energies, and a pressure to commit to the incarnation of our best selves, to what they called the "individuation process." They viewed this archetypal Self as the *imago Dei,* a god-imago in every psyche. Both Jung and Edinger felt a sense of this inner reality as an undomesticated *mysterium tremendum,* a wonderful and terrible reality in the psyche. They believed it to be imperative that we relate to this reality with respect, both consciously and carefully.

Contemporary Jungians all too often trivialize and seek to domesticate this reality and have difficulty understanding that it is the source of the grandiose and exhibitionistic energies in the human psyche. The post-Jungians have sought to question or diminish its reality and significance as a structure in the collective unconscious. Thus they unwittingly enable the dragon to take refuge once again in its increasing invisibility.

Our challenge is to reverse this trend. We must increase our capacity to discern the presence and activities of the dragon. We must break through the enchanted enclosures of consciousness created by our denial and trickster defense mechanisms.

We must give up the arrogant, hopeless attempt to destroy the dragon, for it will be our companion as long as we survive. We must learn to acknowledge it with respect at the same time we disidentify with it. We must resist the temptation to regress into a merger with its beauty and power, its unlimited aspirations and ever-flowing golden energies.

We must, on the other hand, realize that trying to live without the aid of dragon energies condemns us to a dull, depressed, and gray life. People with rigid enough ego-defenses may live out their lives in quiet desperation, but they will seldom experience the golden energies beneath the surface. People with weaker defenses will find the energies manifested in violence, addiction, psychosis, or other archetypal invasions.

The dragon guards the treasures of life. Those who avoid it find their lives drained of energy and creativity. Those who encounter it without conscious intention and good will must know its terrible, horrific face. As Jung suggested, the unconscious meets us in the same spirit that we bring to it.

Thus the only real alternative left to us as individuals and as a species is to face the challenge of a careful, respectful, and conscious befriending of the great dragon within. Jung and Edinger taught us that this is a demanding and perilous path. Development of the relationship must proceed slowly with mutual respect, as with any other serious attempt at deep friendship. Boundaries must be clear and acknowledged. The shadow potentials of each partner must be kept conscious and on the screen while trust is being developed. An arcing of golden energy gradually begins to occur. As the beneficent face of the dragon begins to manifest itself, the radiance of the human partner begins to shine as human potential moves closer to its optimal possibilities.

In summary, we will not realize our potential as individuals or as a species without a conscious and committed effort to befriend the Great Self that presses all of us from within and will continue to assault our dark, depressed little citadels of ego until we open ourselves up to a larger, more radiant life. The strategies of Beowulf and Ahab will not work. Our future turns on how we accept the challenge of creating a conscious, respectful partnership with the dragon. This is the challenge I leave with you.

Diagrams

DIAGRAM 1: THE DEEP STRUCTURES OF THE HUMAN SELF

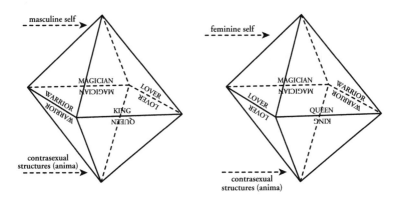

Models of the complete bisexual archetypal Self in octahedral form (the double *quaternio*).

DIAGRAM 2: THE FOUR TENSIONS IN THE HUMAN SELF

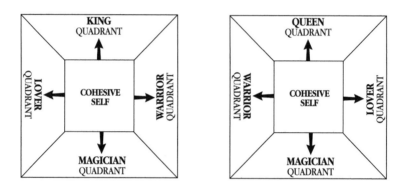

Arrows indicate dialectical tensions built into the deep structure of the psyche and often leading to splitting of the self.

DIAGRAM 3: THE DEVELOPMENTAL JOURNEY TO THE CENTER

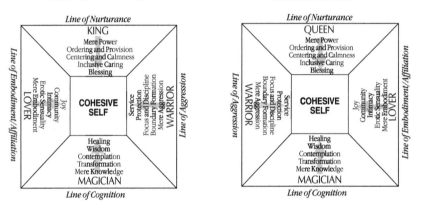

Arrows indicate movement toward integration and cohesion.

Diagram 4: The Geography of Inner Space in Relation to Theodore Millon's Mapping of Psychopathology

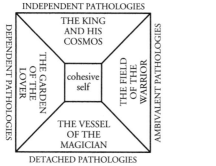

DIAGRAM 5: JOURNEY TO THE CENTER

Chaos   **Chaos**

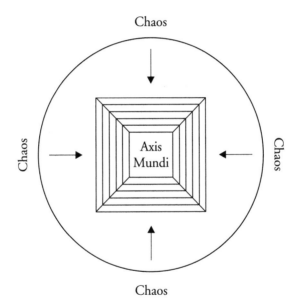

Chaos   **Chaos**

BIBLIOGRAPHY

Adler, Alfred. 1927. *Understanding Human Nature*. W. B. Wolfe, trans. New York: Fawcett. Reprinted: Hazelden, 1998.

_____. 1979. *Superiority and Social Interest: A Collection of Later Writings*. Heinz L. Ansbacher and Rowena R. Ansbacher, eds. Biographical essay by Carl Furtmüller. New York: W. W. Norton.

_____. 1989. *The Individual Psychology of Alfred Adler: A Systematic Presentation in Selections from His Writings*. Heinz L. Ansbacher and Rowena R. Ansbacher, eds. San Francisco: Harper Collins.

American Psychiatric Association Staff. 2000. *Diagnostic and Statistical Manual of Mental Disorders, DSM-IV-TR*. 4th rev. ed. Washington, D.C.: American Psychiatric Association.

Augustine. 1950. *City of God*. Marcus Dods, trans. Introduction by Thomas Morton. New York: Modern Library.

Bailie, Gil. 1995. *Violence Unveiled: Humanity at the Crossroads*. New York: Crossroad Publishing.

Basch, Michael Franz. 1988. *Understanding Psychotherapy: The Science behind the Art*. New York: Basic Books.

_____. 1992. *Practicing Psychotherapy: A Casebook*. New York: Basic Books.

Becker, Alida, ed. 1978. *The Tolkien Scrapbook*. New York: Grosset and Dunlap.

Becker, Ernest. 1968. *The Structure of Evil: An Essay on the Unification of the Science of Man*. New York: Free Press.

_____. 1975. *The Denial of Death*. New York: Free Press.

_____. 1985. *Escape from Evil*. New York: Free Press.

Berger, Peter L. 1967. *The Sacred Canopy: Elements of a Sociological Theory of Religion.* New York: Doubleday.

———. 1969. *A Rumor of Angels: Modern Society and the Rediscovery of the Supernatural.* New York: Doubleday.

———. 1979. *The Heretical Imperative: Contemporary Possibilities of Religious Affirmation.* New York: Doubleday.

Berger, Peter L., Brigitte Berger, and Hansfried Kellner. 1973. *The Homeless Mind.* New York: Random House.

Bly, Robert. 1973. *Sleepers Joining Hands.* New York: Harper. Reprinted: Harper Perennial, 1991.

———. 1990. *Iron John: A Book about Men.* Reading, Mass.: Addison-Wesley.

Bolen, Jean. 1984. *Goddesses in Everywoman: A New Psychology of Women.* New York: Harper and Row.

———. 1989. *Gods in Everyman: A New Psychology of Men's Lives and Loves.* New York: Harper and Row.

Boyd, James W. 1975. *Satan and Mara: Christian and Buddhist Symbols of Evil.* Leiden: E. J. Brill.

Browning, Donald S. 1987. *Religious Thought and Modern Psychology.* Philadelphia: Fortress Press.

Brunner, Thomas M. 2000. A proposed model for comparing writers in the mythopoetic branch of the contemporary men's movement. In *Mythopoetic Perspectives of Men's Healing Work: An Anthology for Therapists and Other.* Edward Read Barton, ed. Westport, Conn.: Bergin and Garvey, pp. 75–86.

Campbell, Joseph. 1949. *The Hero with a Thousand Faces.* Bollingen. Reprinted: Princeton University Press, 1972.

Carpenter, Humphrey. 1977. *Tolkien: A Biography.* Boston: Houghton Mifflin.

Chase, Carole F. 1995. *Madeleine L'Engle, Suncatcher: The Spiritual Vision of a Storyteller.* San Diego: Lura Media.

Coan, R. W. 1984. Complexes. In *Encyclopedia of Psychology.* Raymond J. Corsini, ed. New York: John Wiley, vol. 1, pp. 261–2.

Covey, Stephen R. 1989. *The Seven Habits of Highly Effective People: Restoring the Character Ethic.* New York: Simon and Schuster.

DeBlassie, Paula, III. 1990. *Deep Prayer: Healing for the Hurting Soul.* New York: Crossroad.

Diamond, Jared. 1992. *The Third Chimpanzee: The Evolution and Future of the Human Animal.* San Francisco: HarperCollins.

Dossey, Larry. 1993. *Healing Words: The Power of Prayer and the Practice of Medicine.* San Francisco: Harper.

Dossey, Larry, and Joan Borysenko. 1999. *Science and the Power of Prayer.* Elda Hartley, dir. WinStar Video.

Edinger, Edward F. 1972. *Ego and Archetype: Individuation and the Religious Function of the Psyche.* Kendra Crossen, ed. New York: G. P. Putnam's Sons. Reprinted: Shambhala, 1992.

_____. 1999. *Archetype of the Apocalypse: A Jungian Study of the Book of Revelation.* George R. Elder, ed. Peru, Ill.: Open Court Publishing Co.

Eisler, Riane. 1987. *The Chalice and The Blade.* San Francisco: HarperCollins.

Eliade, Mircea. 1954. *The Myth of the Eternal Return: Cosmos and History.* Willard R. Trask, trans. Princeton, N.J.: Princeton University Press.

_____. 1959. *The Sacred and the Profane: The Nature of Religion.* Willard R. Trask, trans. New York: Harcourt, Brace and World. Reprinted: Harper Torchbooks, 1961.

Elson, Miriam. 1988. *Self Psychology and Clinical Social Work.* New York: W. W. Norton.

Erikson, Erik H. 1959. *Identity and the Life Cycle: Selected Papers.* New York: International Universities Press. Reprinted: W. W. Norton, 1980.

_____. 1963. *Childhood and Society.* New York: W. W. Norton.

_____. 1993. *Gandhi's Truth: On the Origins of Militant Nonviolence.* New York: W. W. Norton.

_____. 2000. *The Erik Erikson Reader.* Robert Coles, ed. New York: W. W. Norton.

Falk, Nancy E. Auer. 1987. Mara. In *The Encyclopedia of Religion.* Mircea Eliade, ed. New York: Macmillan, vol. 9, pp. 187–88.

Forsythe, Neil. 1987. *The Old Enemy: Satan and the Combat Myth.* Princeton, N.J.: Princeton University Press.

Fox, Matthew. 1991. *Creation Spirituality: Liberating Gifts for the Peoples of the Earth.* San Francisco: Harper.

Frankfort, Henri. 1948. *Kingship and the Gods: A Study of a Near Eastern Religion as the Integration of Society and Nature.* Chicago: University of Chicago Press.

Freud, Sigmund. 1961. *Civilization and Its Discontents.* James Strachey, trans. and ed. New York: W. W. Norton. First published in Vienna, 1930.

Gaster, Theodor H., ed. 1964. *The Dead Sea Scriptures.* New York: Anchor Books/Doubleday. Reprinted: Peter Smith, 1993.

Hannah, Barbara. 1981. *Encounters with the Soul: Active Imagination as Developed by C. G. Jung.* Pittsburgh, Pa.: Sigo Press. Reprinted: Chiron, 2001.

_____. 1999. *The Inner Journey: Lectures and Essays on Jungian Psychology.* Dean L. Frantz, ed. Toronto: Inner City Books.

Hazell, Jeremy, ed. 1995. *Personal Relations Therapy: The Collected Papers of H. J. S. Guntrip.* Northvale, N.J.: Jason Aronson.

_____. 1996. *H. J. S. Guntrip: A Psychoanalytical Biography.* London: Free Association Books.

Heaney, Seamus, trans. and ed. 2000. *Beowulf: A New Verse Translation.* New York: Farrar, Straus and Giroux.

Hendrix, Harville. 1988. *Getting the Love You Want: A Guide for Couples.* New York: Henry Holt.

Homans, Peter. 1979. *Jung in Context: Modernity and the Making of a Psychology.* Chicago: University of Chicago Press.

_____. 1989. *The Ability to Mourn: Disillusionment and the Social Origins of Psychoanalysis.* Chicago: University of Chicago Press.

Jacoby, Mario. 1985. *Longing for Paradise: Psychological Perspectives on an Archetype.* Myron Gubitz, trans. Pittsburgh, Pa.: Sigo Press.

Jaynes, Julian. 1978. *The Origin of Consciousness in the Breakdown of the Bicameral Mind.* Toronto: University of Toronto Press. Reprinted: Houghton Mifflin, 1999.

Johnson, Robert. 1985. *We: Understanding the Psychology of Romantic Love*. San Francisco: Harper.

_____. 1986. *Inner Work: Using Dreams and Creative Imagination for Personal Growth and Integration*. San Francisco: Harper.

_____. 1989. *Ecstasy: Understanding the Psychology of Joy*. San Francisco: Harper.

Jonas, Hans. 1958. *The Gnostic Religion*. Boston: Beacon Press.

Jung, Carl G. 1952. *Answer to Job*. R. F. C. Hull, trans. Princeton, N.J.: Princeton University Press, 1973.

_____. 1968. *The Archetypes and the Collective Unconscious*. In *Collected Works*, vol 9/1. Princeton, N.J.: Princeton University Press.

_____. 1969. *The Structure and Dynamics of the Psyche*. In *Collected Works*, vol. 8. Princeton, N.J.: Princeton University Press.

_____. 1996. *On Active Imagination*. New York: Routledge.

Keen, Sam. 1986. *Faces of the Enemy: Reflections of the Hostile Imagination*. San Francisco: Harper and Row.

Kelsey, Morton T. 1974. *God, Dreams, and Revelation*. Minneapolis: Augsburg Press.

_____. 1978. *Dreams: A Way to Listen to God*. New York: Paulist Press.

_____. 1988. *Encounter with God*. New York: Paulist Press.

Klein, Melanie. 1984. *Envy and Gratitude, and Other Works, 1946–1963*. *The Writings of Melanie Klein*, vol. 3. New York: Free Press.

Kohut, Heinz. 1971. *The Analysis of the Self: A Systematic Approach to the Psychoanalytic Treatment of Narcissistic Personality Disorders*. New York: International Universities Press.

_____. 1985. *Self Psychology and the Humanities: Reflections on a New Psychoanalytic Approach*. Charles B. Strozier, ed. New York: W. W. Norton.

Lammers, Ann. 1994. *In God's Shadow: The Collaboration of Victor White and C. G. Jung*. Mahwah, N.J.: Paulist Press.

Lee, Ronald, et al. 1991. *Psychotherapy after Kohut*. Hillsdale, N. J.: Analytic Press.

L'Engle, Madeleine. 1997. *Madeleine L'Engle's Time Quartet*, 4 vols. New York: Dell.

Leonard, Linda Schierse. 1986. *On the Way to the Wedding: Transforming the Love Relationship*. New York: Random House.

Levin, Jerome D. 1987. *Treatment of Alcoholism and Other Addictions: A Self Psychology Approach*. Northvale, N.J.: Aronson.

_____. 1993. *Slings and Arrows: Narcissistic Injury and Its Treatment*. Northvale, N.J.: Aronson.

Lewis, C. S. 1942. *The Screwtape Letters*. London.

Ling, Trevor O. 1962. *Buddhism and the Mythology of Evil: A Study in Theravada Buddhism*. Boston: Oneworld, 1997.

Meckel, Daniel J., and Robert L. Moore, eds. 1992. *Self and Liberation: The Jung-Buddhism Dialogue*. New York: Paulist Press.

Melton, J. Gordon, and Martin Baumann, eds. 2002. *Religions of the World: A Comprehensive Encyclopedia of Beliefs and Practices*. Santa Barbara, Calif.: ABC-Clio.

Miller, Dean A. 2000. *The Epic Hero*. Baltimore: Johns Hopkins University Press.

Millon, Theodore. 1969. *Modern Psychopathology*. Philadelphia: Saunders. Reprinted Prospect Heights, Ill.: Waveland Press, 1985.

Moore, Robert L. 1979. *John Wesley and Authority: A Psychological Perspective*. Missoula, Mont.: Scholars Press.

_____. 1984. Space and transformation in human experience. In *Anthropology and the Study of Religion*, Robert L. Moore and Frank Reynolds, eds. Chicago: Center for the Scientific Study of Religion, pp. 126–43.

_____. 1996. The self and the shadow of the healer: Perspectives from structural psychoanalysis. In *Healing and the Healer*, George F. Cairns, Lawrence A. Pottenger, and Nancy U. Cairns, eds. Chicago: Exploration Press, pp. 163–78.

_____. 2001. *The Archetype of Initiation: Sacred Space, Ritual Process, and Personal Transformation*. Max J. Havlick, Jr., ed. Philadelphia: Xlibris.

_____. 2002. *The Magician and the Analyst: The Archetype of the Magus in Occult Spirituality and Jungian Analysis*. Philadelphia: Xlibris.

Moore, Robert L., ed. 1988. *Carl Jung and Christian Spirituality*. New York: Paulist Press.

Moore, Robert, and Douglas Gillette. 1989. The last rite. Unpublished manuscript.

_____. 1990. *King Warrior Magician Lover: Rediscovering the Archetypes of the Mature Masculine Personality.* San Francisco: Harper Collins.

_____. 1991. *The King Within: Accessing the King in the Male Psyche.* New York: William Morrow.

_____. 1992. *The Warrior Within: Accessing the Knight in the Male Psyche.* New York: William Morrow.

_____. 1993a. *The Lover Within: Accessing the Lover in the Male Psyche.* New York: William Morrow.

_____. 1993b. *The Magician Within: Accessing the Shaman in the Male Psyche.* New York: William Morrow.

Moore, Robert L., and Daniel J. Meckel, eds. 1990. *Jung and Christianity in Dialogue.* New York: Paulist Press.

Moss, Robert. 1996. *Conscious Dreaming: A Spiritual Path for Everyday Life.* New York: Crown.

Niebuhr, Reinhold. 1941–1943. *The Nature and Destiny of Man,* 2 vols. New York: Scribners.

Pagels, Elaine. 1979. *The Gnostic Gospels.* New York: Random House.

Parkin, David J., ed. 1985. *Anthropology and Evil.* Oxford: Blackwell.

Partin, Harry Baxter. 1967. The Muslim pilgrimage: Journey to the center. Ph.D. dissertation, University of Chicago Divinity School.

Perry, John Weir. 1953. *The Self in Psychotic Process: Its Symbolization in Schizophrenia.* Woodstock, Conn.: Spring Publications, 1987.

_____. 1966. *The Lord of the Four Quarters: Myths of the Royal Father.* New York: Braziller. Reprinted as *Lord of the Four Quarters: The Mythology of Kingship.* New York: Paulist Press, 1991.

_____. 1976. *Roots of Renewal in Myth and Madness.* San Francisco: Jossey-Bass.

_____. 1987. *The Heart of History: Individuality in Evolution.* Albany, N.Y.: State University of New York Press.

Quenk, Alex T., and Naomi L. Quenk. 1995. *Dream Thinking: The Logic, Magic, and Meaning of Your Dreams.* Palo Alto, Calif.: Davies-Black.

FACING THE DRAGON

Randall, Robert L. 1988. *Pastor and Parish: The Psychological Core of Ecclesiastical Conflicts.* New York: Human Sciences Press.

Rauer, Christine. 2000. *Beowulf and the Dragon: Parallels and Analogues.* Cambridge: D. S. Brewer.

Remarque, Erich-Maria. 1930. *All Quiet on the Western Front.* A. W. Wheen, trans. Boston: Little Brown.

Robinson, James, ed. 1990. *The Nag Hammadi Library in English,* rev. ed. San Francisco: Harper.

Rogers, David J. 1988. *Waging Business Warfare.* New York: Kensington.

Russell, Jeffery Burton. 1977. *The Devil: Perceptions of Evil from Antiquity to Primitive Christianity.* Ithaca, N.Y.: Cornell University Press.

_____. 1981. *Satan: The Early Christian Tradition.* Ithaca, N.Y.: Cornell University Press.

_____. 1984. *Lucifer: The Devil in the Middle Ages.* Ithaca, N.Y.: Cornell University Press.

_____. 1986. *Mephistopheles: The Devil in the Modern World.* Ithaca, N.Y.: Cornell University Press.

Sanford, John A. 1968. *Dreams: God's Forgotten Language.* Philadelphia: Lippincott. Reprinted: Crossroad, 1984.

_____. 1987. *The Strange Case of Mr. Hyde: A New Look at the Nature of Human Evil.* San Francisco: Harper and Row.

Schultz, Jeffrey D., and John G. West, Jr., eds. 1998. *The C. S. Lewis Readers' Encyclopedia.* Grand Rapids, Mich.: Zondervan.

Shanahan, Margaret L. 1994. Psychological perspectives on vampire mythology. In *The Vampire Book: The Encyclopedia of the Undead.* J. Gordon Melton, ed. Detroit: Gale Research Press, pp. 492–501.

Singer, June. 1987. Jung's gnosticism and contemporary gnosis. In *Jung's Challenge to Contemporary Religion,* Murray Stein and Robert L. Moore, eds. Wilmette, Ill.: Chiron, pp. 73–92.

Stein, Murray. 1995. *C. G. Jung on Evil.* London: Routledge.

Stein, Murray, and Robert L. Moore, eds. 1987. *Jung's Challenge to Contemporary Religion.* Wilmette, Ill.: Chiron Publications.

Stevens, Anthony. 1982. *Archetypes: A Natural History of the Self.* New York: William Morrow.

_____. 1989. *The Roots of War: A Jungian Perspective.* St. Paul, Minn.: Paragon House.

_____. 1993. *The Two Million-Year-Old Self.* College Station, Texas: Texas A&M Press. Reprinted: Fromm International, 1997.

Strozier, Charles B. 2001. *Heinz Kohut: The Making of a Psychoanalyst.* New York: Farrar, Straus and Giroux.

Sullivan, Harry Stack. 1953. *The Interpersonal Theory of Psychiatry.* Helen Swick Perry and Mary Ladd Gawel, eds. New York: W. W. Norton.

Tillich, Paul. 1952. *The Courage to Be.* New Haven, Conn.: Yale University Press.

_____. 1954. *Love, Power, and Justice.* New York: Oxford University Press.

_____. 1957. *Systematic Theology,* 3 vols. Chicago: University of Chicago Press.

_____. 1984. *The Meaning of Health: Essays in Existentialism, Psychoanalysis, and Religion.* Perry LeFevre, ed. Chicago: Exploration Press.

Turner, Victor W. 1969. *The Ritual Process: Structure and Anti-Structure.* Ithaca, N.Y.: Cornell University Press.

_____. 1973. The center out there: Pilgrim's goal. *History of Religions* 12:191–230.

Turner, Victor W., and Edith Turner. 1978. *Image and Pilgrimage in Christian Culture.* New York: Columbia University Press.

Ulanov, Ann Belford, and Barry Ulanov. 1983. *Cinderella and Her Sisters: The Envied and the Envying.* Philadelphia: Westminster.

_____. 2000. *The Healing Imagination: The Meeting of Psyche and Soul.* Einseideln: Daimon Verlag.

Vermes, Geza. 1995. *The Dead Sea Scrolls in English.* Rev. 4th ed. New York: Penguin Books.

_____. 1997. *The Complete Dead Sea Scrolls in English.* New York: Viking Penguin.

_____. 2000. *Introduction to the Complete Dead Sea Scrolls.* Minneapolis: Augsburg Fortress.

Vladescu, F. V., ed. 1997. Envy. *Journal of Melanie Klein and Object Relations*, vol. 15.

von Franz, Marie-Louise. 1974. *Shadow and Evil in Fairy Tales*. Zurich: Spring.

Waite, Robert G. L. 1977. *The Psychopathic God: Adolf Hitler*. New York: Basic Books.

Walsh, Chad. 1979. *The Literary Legacy of C. S. Lewis*. New York: Harcourt Brace Jovanovich.

Williams, James G. 1991. *The Bible, Violence, and the Sacred: Liberation from the Myth of Sanctioned Violence*. San Francisco: Harper. Reprinted: Trinity Press, 1995.

Wilson, A. N. 1990. *C. S. Lewis: A Biography*. New York: W. W. Norton.

Wolf, Ernest S. 1988. *Treating the Self: Elements of Clinical Self Psychology*. New York: Guilford.

Wright, Robert. 1994. *The Moral Animal: The New Science of Evolutionary Psychology*. New York: Pantheon Books.

Wytenbroek, J. R., with Roger C. Schlobin. 1995. *Nothing Is Ordinary: The Extraordinary Vision of Madeleine L'Engle*. San Bernadino, Calif.: Borgo Press.

INDEX

Boldface page numbers refer to the primary discussion of the topic.

ABOUT THE AUTHOR

Robert L. Moore is Professor of Psychoanalysis, Culture, and Spirituality at the Chicago Theological Seminary where he is the senior professor in the Center for Theology, Ethics, and the Human Sciences. He is a founder and president of the Institute for Psychoanlaysis, Culture, and Spirituality in Chicago.

Dr. Moore is one of the few psychoanalysts in the world who has studied comparative psychoanalytic theory and practice in depth, receiving a diploma in more than one psychoanalytic tradition. His work on neo-Jungian structural psychoanalysis, decoding the structures of the human self, has brought him international recognition as a major psychoanalytic theorist.

In addition to his practice of psychoanalysis and psychoanalytic psychotherapy, he also teaches and has served as a training analyst at the C. G. Jung Institute of Chicago. He lectures widely in the United States and abroad on topics relating to psychoanalysis, ethics, and human spirituality. He is also in demand as an executive coach and consultant in leadership and organizational development to business and government.

Author and editor of numerous books in the field of psychology, psychoanalysis, and spirituality, he is editor of the Paulist Press series on Jungian psychoanalysis and World Spiritual Traditions, an interdisciplinary series relating psychoanalytic insight to the major traditions of human spirituality.

Robert Moore is perhaps most widely known for his work on ritual process and the masculine psyche. His five-volume series on masculine psychology and spirituality (co-authored with mythologist Douglas Gillette) is the most influential theory of masculinity in today's international discussion. The structural psychoanalysis outlined in these books put him at the forefront of theory in masculine psychology, masculine spirituality, and masculine initiation.

A comprehensive list of his audiotaped lectures and books on psychology and spirituality is available through the C. G. Jung Institute of Chicago (847) 475-4848. For other information, you may consult his Web page at www.robertmoore-phd.com. Consultations may be arranged by calling him at (773) 288-7474 or by faxing him at (773) 288-7276 or by emailing him at robertmoore@robertmoorephd.com.

To be informed of forthcoming publications and training events led by Dr. Moore, you may visit his Web page at www.robertmoore-phd.com.